Superheroes
Pagans & Deities

Evolution of the Eastern Mediterranean's Great Faiths

Mystery, Myth & Mystique

Karl C. Hendrixsen

All rights reserved.
No part of this publication may be reproduced in any form or by any means, electronic, mechanical, recording, photocopying, or otherwise, without the prior written permission of the publisher, except for the purpose of authorized published review.

First Edition

Copyright © 2010 by Corystevens Publishing, LLC

Library of Congress Catalogue Number: 2010926282

ISBN: 0-942893076

Printed in the United States of America

www.corystevens.com

Cover photo courtesy of hubblesite.org
Space Telescope Science Institute

Contents

	Introduction	5
1	Early Cultural Evolution	11
2	The Origins of Regional Monotheism	27
3	Babylon & Canaan During the Time of Abraham	30
4	Egypt Around the Time Period of 1600 BCE	34
5	Egyptian Exodus Mystery	42
6	The Ten Plagues of Egypt	51
7	Geologic Causes of the Ten Plagues of Egypt	57
8	The Conflicting Stories of Joseph	63
9	Successor to Moses and Mystery of the Promised Land	67
10	Egypt's Centrist Position for Early Religion	75
11	The Semitic Contribution to Egyptian Monotheism	77
12	Akhenaten, the Heretic King	80
13	Power Surge to Restore Egyptian Paganism	94
14	The Rush to End Monotheism in Ancient Egypt	99
15	Historical Transcendence to a Universal God	106
16	Israelite Prophets and Prophecy	114
17	The Divinity of Jesus Christ	120
18	Islam	129
19	Creation Myths	134
20	The Afterlife of Myth and Religion	147
21	Egyptian Gods and Goddesses	152
22	The Hittites	163
23	Sumerian/Akkadian Gods	171
24	Greek Gods and Goddesses	174
25	Roman Gods and Goddesses	178
26	Scandinavian Gods and Goddesses	183
27	Aztec Gods	187
	Conclusion	189
	Bibliography	197
	Journey Up the Nile	202
	Index	219

Eastern Mediterranean

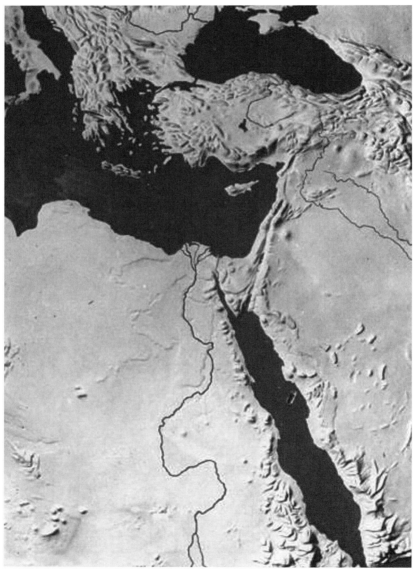

Orographical map by Hans Wild, Time & Life Pictures, January 1, 1940

Introduction

Superman started out as a comic book character created by Joe Shuster and Jerry Siegel during the economic upheavals of the 1930s. The model for the character had distinct roots in the concept of the Aryan super-race that was being perpetrated on the Germanic youth of Europe, the "return to the glories of the Roman Empire" movement of Italy, and the Ninja/Samurai resurgence of Japan. The financial times were extraordinarily tough and the term "depression" reflected the economy and the psyche of much of the world's population. Therefore, an alternative to doom and gloom in the form of a modern superhero was invented and had broad appeal. Along with a dual identity, the secular creation of Superman was human in virtually every respect but was actually a humanoid superhero from the planet Krypton. His appearance, behavior, and, of course, his language were quite acceptable to English-speaking audiences, especially preteen boys. Superman naturally possessed superhuman skills that were used only for positive (good not evil) purposes. Communication with him during a crisis required mental telepathy, prayer, or simple hope that he would intervene due to his own special awareness that was beyond human comprehension. Superman possessed a widely known vulnerability (kryptonite), like Achilles' vulnerable tendon, that evil-doers could use temporarily to strip him of his superior powers but not actually kill him. The unstated impression was that Superman, once here, would live forever, not age, and always be on the side of "peace, justice, and the American way."

In much earlier times such a squeaky-clean hero would likely evolve into a local, regional, or perhaps worldly god to be placated, honored, respected, feared, blamed, and ultimately be put into conflict with other competing gods. This juxtaposition of the gods and goddesses would further imitate humanity with all of the nuances of family including adultery, neglect, abuse, incest, abandonment, adoption, and disproportionate punishment or reward. Early gods, especially Sumerian gods, reflected the entire family with husbands and wives, children, grandparents, in-laws, consorts, and other relatives until there was an entire pantheon of divine superhumans with known capabilities, limitations, and the full range of human emotions on a grander scale. Given the limitless boundaries of literary imagination, Superman could magically morph into another being, such as Superwoman or Superboy. New superheroes rapidly evolved such as Bat Man and Bat Boy, Wonder Woman, the Green Hornet, Mighty Mouse, the Incredible Hulk, Mutant Ninja Turtles, and other characters as diverse as the human imagination. It is also important to recognize that superheroes do not age and do not experience consequences in the same way as humans. How many times has Wylie Coyote been smashed to oblivion only to come back again and again? Superheroes do not get ill and rarely, if ever, die. The animated superhero is created for entertainment value and the obvious commercial value of selling spin-offs, knock-offs, and creating commercial desires, or at least holding one's attention long enough to instill a commercial desire. Few adults would anticipate that non-animated versions of Superman or Batman would transcend from the secular to the sacred because of the super-sophistication of our times. The child raised in the ancient village, however, with few or typically no validity checks for fanciful stories, was predisposed to accept mythological characters as real.

Human imaginations, in all of their diversity, are limited to a large extent by the certainty of control by others and the historical or cultural context of their present realities. Events that occur within specific time frames are typically within a fixed context. A devastating flood that destroyed the city of Atlantis, for instance, conceivably destroyed the evidence that the fabled city actually existed. Real floods throughout human history could also be embellished with a fanciful tale of the city of Atlantis that is strictly a product of the rich human imagination. For nearly all of early human history and prehistory, travel was limited to distances that could be covered on foot, with the assistance of a large mammal such as a horse, or with a flotation device ranging from a raft to a sailing ship. Two hundred years ago, for instance, most humans could only travel at the walking pace of perhaps four miles per hour, a bit faster with the assistance of a horse, or faster yet with the force of the wind aboard a sailing ship. In 1809 Napoleon and his opponents were dependent upon horse-drawn artillery, cavalry, swords, and muskets.

On one coincidental day 200 years ago on February 12, 1809, two men were born who would have tremendous impacts on a world that was still quite technologically deficient. Their names were Charles Darwin and Abraham Lincoln. Their impact on the present world is immeasurable. At the peaks of their careers, however, the rudiments of electronic communication were barely in place. Rail travel was a recent innovation and automobiles, airplanes, telephones, and high-speed communication did not exist, except for the telegraph. Actually, the telegraph was so new at the outbreak of the Civil War in the United States that Lincoln saw its merits immediately and acknowledged the lightning-like speed of communication as a method "...harnessed to take this man's tidings in a trifle less than no time." His same birth-date compatriot, Charles Darwin, stated in *The Origin of Species* in 1859 that, "To suppose that the eye with all its inimitable contrivances for adjusting the focus to different distances, for admitting different amounts of light, and for the correction of spherical and chromatic aberration, could have been formed by natural selection, seems, I confess, absurd in the highest degree."

Each age has produced superheroes and even super-villains of one sort or another who exist somewhere in the public's consciousness and impact our lives in ways that we do not tend to think about much and may not even acknowledge. Prior to Johann Gutenberg's development of movable type on a printing press, for instance, books were usually copied by hand and were extremely rare, costly, and virtually unavailable to the public, who were mostly illiterate. Now, books and items in print are so prevalent that they are often considered valueless and a source of concern for filling up landfills and using paper pulp sources to such an extent that our forests are becoming completely depleted. The ancients who faced a virtually zero-tech world had other issues related to coming of age, reproducing, being self-supporting, being safe, and eventually passing on to an uncertain afterlife. All of the gaps in knowledge about origins, causes, effects, illnesses, tragedies, blessings, and worlds beyond this world had to be filled with something. That something, although continuing to evolve, has been the product of the human imagination. Given some factual context such as an actual event, the mind fills in the blank spaces. Transmission by oral tradition, fanciful art, sculpture, and architecture did much of the rest. The folklore, mythologies, art, temples, discoveries, and all traces of what survives combine to be a blend of the world's treasure of knowledge and belief. History is typically written from the point of view of those in authority at the time and by the winners of momentous struggles. Groups of people who no longer exist, for whatever reason, have little or no legacy to pass forward. Their life experiences, art, music, poetry, literature, mythologies, religion, gods, superheroes, and villains are mostly or completely forgotten. As languages become extinct, most or all of the folklore and history associated with that language dies as well. This book is intended to be an acknowledgement of the power and pervasiveness of mythology, the power and diversity of the human imagination, and a tribute to memories and experiences of the past and those who, rightly or wrongly, preceded us and left their mark.

Phoenician Goddess c. 2500 BCE

"Angry Horus" at the Temple of Edfu

1
Early Cultural Evolution

> Carbon-14 dating doesn't work on rocks, but find something organic, such as an ancient stick handle attached, and it does.

History evolves with new information, new perspectives, new writers, and time. The earliest history is drawn from surviving written records in hieroglyphs, cuneiform, Mayan glyphs, and remnants of languages that have long ago died out or have evolved enough to be barely recognizable to the most skilled linguists. Earliest recorded history, including petroglyphs, ancient burial sites, wall paintings inside caves and tombs, remnants of architecture, and any surviving artifacts of human activities, is combined with oral histories and perhaps committed to written records. Due to the destructiveness of natural forces, information about prehistoric human activity requires extensive inferences and cross-referencing when possible. Later, with the invention of writing, the earliest scribes were likely among the very few to be allowed to acquire literacy skills and they served at the pleasure of authoritarian figures with their own agendas to serve. Objectivity has not been the standard for recording events. Human intelligence and imagination have always been present, and scribes generally risked banishment or death for failing to serve the special interest of their masters. The biggest difference between "us" and "them" is our acquired knowledge base (or at least access to geometrically growing knowledge bases). Our ancient ancestors were otherwise fully representative of the present. They were mostly hard-working people with good intentions doing what they needed to do to support and raise their families. There were also scoundrels, thieves, slackers, manipulators, those who would exploit others for their own personal gain, and all of the variations of human behavior that has been evidenced in the past.

"In the beginning...." is one of those all-inclusive, unchallenged introductions that convey an image of a cold planet, devoid of life, orbiting a dormant sun. Divine intervention at some point in time sets everything that we presently know about the earth and universe into play as it is known today. Can our very existence be explained by a series of superhuman events? Each culture has framed the question of origins with colorful, mythological stories that were orally passed to succeeding generations. Repetition has allowed the gifted great storytellers to embellish and refine such tales and make them an integral part of their culture. Early Egyptians, for one, viewed the origins of the earth as a bubbling sea of mud under the influence of chaotic forces of nature. Eventually an island emerged that allowed the beginning formation of the plant and animal life that we see today. Of course, this new environment was divided by and annually controlled by the northerly flow of the world's longest river-the Nile. The creation myth of the ancient Egyptian city of Heliopolis viewed the earth and sky as anthropomorphic deities with Geb as the god of the earth and Nut arching herself over Geb as the goddess of the sky. The creation myth of Memphis, ancient capital of Egypt beginning with the First Dynasty (c. 3100 BCE), centered on the priests' supreme deity, Ptah (pay-tah'). This god was described as the "father of all gods," and the source of all life. He created the universe within his heart and created all other deities. He created all living things by declaring their names. To accomplish such feats Ptah harnessed divine energy (heka), divine knowledge (sia), and divine utterance (hu). The primordial theme within the Egyptian creation story was the imposition of order over chaos. The result was a protocivilization within the Nile Valley that was willing to make supreme sacrifices to preserve order in place of chaos, and the result of such effort was a superior civilization that survived for thousands of years.

Which Came First, the Chicken or the Egg?

From a practical view of Earth's origins, there has never been a complex plant or animal born without a mature precedent. Identifying the absolute first "mature precedent" of any given species is impossible because it can never be documented. The only possible exception would be the introduction of an entirely new organism, nurturing that new organism to sexual maturity, and then observing the very first generation of reproduction. Put in another way, no living organism has ever progressed from birth to maturity without an adult equivalent being present to pass on its genetic code and, in the case of higher-level organisms, to pass along at least some hint of survival skills as well. For all species of mammals, the moment of birth was either successful or it was not. In the case of humans, actual birth was typically assisted by midwife relatives and companions who may have had some prior experience. Childbirth was typically not a solitary experience, and not always a successful experience. Infant mortality rates in all ancient cultures have been high. From the moment of birth the new infant is cared for and will typically learn virtually everything it needs to survive and to mature into the next generation from the immediate parents, other family, and companions who are present. The infant will eventually acquire language skills and other behaviors through imitation of the small cluster of adults and perhaps other children in its immediate environment. The worldliness acquired by the infant is almost totally limited to what it is able to observe and imitate of the people in its day-to-day surroundings. The focus of the earliest days was typically upon the most rudimentary elements of obtaining enough nourishment for survival, protection from the elements, and basic safety skills to increase the potential for survival at least to the next generation. Incredibly, little changed for many thousands of years at a time. Humans differed little from other social animals who shared their environment. The times of darkness, when the sun had set each day, may have been opportunities to ruminate about questions of origins, purposes, and explanation of events out of the ordinary. The first line of communication of culture and world view was most likely from the mother to the young child and supplemented by others within the family, the multigenerational group, the small group or clan that stuck together to bring children into an adult life.

The 1.5-Million-Year-Old Footprint

As scientific investigations continue to reset the clock for human habitation, Ann Gibbons reported in *ScienceNOW Daily News* (26 February 2009) on human footprints discovered in what is now Ileret, Kenya, dating back as much as 1.5 million years. The images that have been preserved in clay-like soil that became rock were believed to have been left by an early species of Homo erectus and show the large toe being parallel with the other toes, an indication of an upright stride. Footprints discovered in Laetoli, Tanzania, and dating back approximately 3.75 million years belonged to an upright human species known as australopithecines who had a more simian type of large toe that slanted away from the others.

Chimpanzees, in contrast, have had an equivalent or greater number of successive generations than humans, yet their behavior has changed little for hundreds of thousands of years. Each generation did not consistently build on the experiences of the previous generation and move on to new levels. Similar behaviors were simply repeated again and again to the extent that external conditions remained about the same. Most of early human history was comparable and a time-consuming struggle to maintain food and shelter. By assuming an average of 25 years for each generation and a period of up to one million years, there were at least 40,000 generations of humans, but only in the last 10,000 years have human knowledge and technological capabilities increased at a geometric rate. The most notable differences beginning approximately 10 millennia ago were in diversity of knowledge and language, not intelligence. Oral and nonverbal traditions within each family, clan, or small group probably took on great significance in the form of learning and preserving stories, acquiring daily living skills, providing entertainment to quell anxieties, discomforts, or boredom, and communicating the adult point of view no matter how crude, misinformed, or erroneous. Scientific evidence has demonstrated that the diversity of intelligence of our ancient ancestors is very much equivalent to that of our own present times, but for obvious reasons their intellectual development was haunted by superstitions, biases, and extreme limits on their knowledge of the world as we know it today.

Early Technology and Innovation

The earliest transition from a nomadic hunter-gatherer existence with little potential for cultural evolution or change occurred along the Nile River Valley and the river valleys of the Tigris, Euphrates, Jordan, and lesser bodies of fresh water in what would later be northeastern Africa and the Middle East. The cultural evolution within the region was more or less simultaneous because physical proximity was near enough for both economic and social trade. Wild grass seeds in ancient times were likely selected (domesticated) and harvested on the basis of larger and larger edible seeds. Concentrations of these seeds were planted in much the same way that the seeds dispersed themselves naturally, and they were cultivated with supplemental irrigation and very warm growing seasons. More reliable supplements to the ancient hunting and gleaning diet necessitated a more sedentary lifestyle. Increased potential to feed and domesticate animals for consumption would have existed for the first time. This phenomenon in early human development is especially well described in Jared Diamond's excellent books entitled *The Third Chimpanzee* and *Guns, Germs and Steel*. Potential was greatly increased as a result of larger populations, diversification of work tasks, and solutions to needs for more permanent housing, food storage, sewage disposal, protection from marauders, and solutions to the evolving complications of increasing numbers of people, increased crops, and growing numbers of domestic animals living in close proximity. Among the urgent changes for living in cities, i.e., "civilization," would be new rules for behavior, consequences for transgressions, new distributions of labor, hierarchies of power and authority, care for the sick, care for children, care for the elderly, and care for the dead.

The Formation of Small Villages

Evolving from the late Stone Age with its emphasis on kiln-fired pottery, sun-dried bricks, and use of domestic beasts of burden, crude irrigation, and stone-tipped weapons, early people in the region likely formed common alliances in small communities to care for each other and to look after each other's interests in ways to sustain their community. One of the earliest settlements to become established (actually over and over again with one layer on top of more ancient layers) was the city of Jericho located between Mt. Nebo in the east, the Central Mountains in the west, the Dead Sea to the south and bordering the Jordan

River. Dating back as far as 8,000 BCE, Jericho represents one of humanity's earliest settlements in the transition from nomadic to agrarian existence and has been the site of roughly 23 identifiable layers of different cultural habitations built one on top of another to the present date. Jericho was at the crossroads of early trade and ethnic/religious rivalries. Key geographical positioning meant that ideas as well as tangible goods and services were exchanged along those frequented trade routes.

6,500-Year-Old Village Found in Central Greece

As recently as 2008, archaeologists discovered the ruins of an ancient farming village in central Greece. Among the new finds were the remains of houses constructed with wood and clay. Also found were remnants of clay vases, ovens, and some stone tools.

The new find dates to the Neolithic Era which preceded the Early Bronze Age, and was accidentally discovered as a pipe-laying crew was digging near the village of Vassili in the province of Thessaly, about 170 miles north of the present city of Athens. The site is located within a fertile plain that was attractive to many of the world's first agrarian people of that region and just one of perhaps 300 different settlements that have been rediscovered in Greece within the last 200 years. The village near Vassili showed evidence of being destroyed by a fire that served to harden the clay components of the structures and to preserve imprints of the structural wood elements. Also found were large quantities of broken pottery with some pieces still showing the glazed images that had been added, bone and stone tools and utensils such as scrappers, stone axes, and even a small number of terracotta figurines that are distinct indicators of art and religion.

Cultural Evolution

Among the deductions that can be made from the find described above is that settled village life supported by farming as well as hunting and gleaning was a commonplace reality. Multi-generational groups were living together in sheltered housing with cooking and food preparation tools, and the means of storing water, fruit juices, and perhaps beer and wine. Midwifery and medical treatment were being provided with only the most rudimentary, primitive, trial-and-error knowledge of sanitation, surgery, and even the means to treat bodily infections except through the body's own defenses. Light after sunset was limited to the continually changing stages of the moon, firelight, and the potential candle. The small clusters of people huddled in small shelters, compared to modern housing, had many hours each evening to recount experiences with nature and other people. The most authoritarian and perhaps the most imaginative people had captive audiences for weaving tall tales to account for life's experiences plus the mysterious and unexplained aspects of day-to-day life. Oral traditions would have held much sway over children, and subordinate adults, and would be the major diversion along with preparation tasks, eating, and sleeping. Stories retold again and again through many generations had great potential for embellishment, refinement, and for mesmerizing a typically captive audience. In addition, clay, chipped stone, or terracotta figurines and line art had great potential for attributing superhero and perhaps magical powers to explain life's diverse and infinite mysteries.

A far more recent discovery, dating to approximately 640 BCE, has just been unearthed near Saqqara, Egypt. A virtual storeroom of mummies, as described by Egypt's archaeology chief, Zahi Hawass, contained eight wooden and limestone sarcophagi and almost two dozen previously undisturbed mummies. Zahi described the period as the Twenty-Sixth Dynasty and the time of Egypt's last independent kingdom before falling to a succession of foreign conquerors. The find, early in the year 2009, is especially important because Saqqara, just 12 miles south of Cairo, is the site where ancient rulers of the Egyptian capital of Memphis were buried. This may be just one of many ancient sites to be discovered. This new discovery is especially significant because the old capital of Memphis has been demolished beyond recognition except for a very few carved stone remnants.

Early Human Settlements and Survival

DNA combined with archeology, carbon-14 dating, and evolutionary/scientific studies to date place the origins of the human species on the continent of Africa. Richard Leakey's discovery of Australopithecus africanus (Lucy) consisted of the minimal remains of a roughly 4-foot tall adult female dating back over 3 million years. She obviously did not live alone and did have human characteristics in her surviving bone and dental structure. The small clan that she was a part of probably subsisted on grassy plains and survived by remaining in the vicinity of wooded streams and rivers, not the open plains. The small clusters of nomadic descendants of Lucy probably changed very little for hundreds of thousands of years in a warm region rich in edible plant life, carrion from animal kills, plus fish, fowl, reptiles, and mammals that they were able to trap or kill. Lifespans were usually quite short due to the potential for death from injuries, disease, starvation, childbirth complications, and possibly being the prey of human or wild animal predators. Archeological evidence suggests that lifespans much beyond early sexual reproduction were rare, and children, especially orphaned ones, were likely to be raised by the nomadic group, not just the immediate family. Scientific evidence has demonstrated that intelligence was comparable to that of humans today, yet the world knowledge these early humans possessed was only slightly removed from other predatory omnivores. One clear-cut distinction was the extensive use of fire and of oral sounds to communicate and to describe all facets of life. Language and various art forms were especially useful to explain the unknown in ways that made some degree of sense. Gods of fertility, for example, have been among the earliest figurines discovered at ancient gravesites, and it can only be implied that the mysteries of reproduction were revered and likely associated with rituals to give thanks and to preserve whatever was making childbirth possible. Reproductive acts were readily observed among most other species of animals and childbirth, and early nurturing was likely to be partly instinctive and partly a result of imitation of others within their small group and the animal world around them.

Migration was a prevalent feature of early human existence to ensure at least a subsistence-level diet. Frequent relocation was also necessary to avoid depleting edible substances, to avoid smelly contamination of water and soil, and to reduce the potential of being the victim of predators. Bathing in clean water may or may not have been practiced except by accidental transfer across streams or other bodies of water. The use of odors to identify edible from inedible material was probably far more sensitive in the ancient world than present life where so much is sanitized, packaged, scented, refrigerated, frozen, canned, freeze-dried, or dehydrated. Bacteria and viruses were not identified until the seventeenth century with the first development of a microscope by Antony van Leeuwenhoek in 1673. Practical inferences throughout most of history prior to that time were likely made on the basis of decaying flesh of the dead and infected flesh of the living. Actually, it was not until the discovery and development of penicillin prior to World War II that severely injured soldiers did not die of infections that followed their battlefield wounds. Originally, a French medical student, Ernest Duchesne, in 1897 noticed the beneficial effects of penicillin mold. In 1928 a Scottish researcher, Sir Alexander Fleming, advanced the research, but it was not until the early 1940s that Howard Florey and Ernst Chain were able to isolate the active ingredient of penicillin and to convert it to a powdery medicine that has saved countless lives.

Early Civilizations and Migration Patterns

Migrating humans were inclined to follow rivers and streams due to the inability to carry large volumes of drinkable water along with all other necessities of life on their own backs and sometimes on the backs of domesticated beasts of burden. Major rivers, such as the Nile, were of such great size that large numbers of family/clan/groups could coexist without frequently coming into conflict with each other, or of contaminating the moving waters. Migratory behavior could adapt to variations such as periodic floods, seasonal weather variations, droughts, animal migrations, range fires, and pressures from competing groups. One of the more natural migrations would be with the northward flow of the Nile because some possessions could be floated with the current along a course of thousands of miles that eventually fans into fertile delta lands and empties into the Mediterranean Sea. The land northward from the Nile Delta could be traversed by following the Mediterranean coastline and dispersing to the northeast and northwest as the last Ice Age receded and edible plants and animals could again be found or cultivated. The earliest nomads, the proto-Egyptian peoples, occupied a fragile river valley with fertile soil on both sides and inhospitable desert beyond the narrow band of fertile soil. One of the natural inclinations to evolve was a magical or spiritual feeling about the sun rising in the east each day with a regularity that would be attributed to the daily birth of a deity and followed by the daily death on the western horizon where little or nothing survived. The sun was such an important feature of Egyptian daily life that became their most important god for thousands of years. Also, the early Egyptians had an "up close and personal" relationship with their gods. The gods often had conflicts of their own. Some married and had children and in general exhibited human foibles as well as superhuman abilities. A very complex pantheon of gods and goddesses was the result, and early Egyptians believed that certain rituals had to be endlessly performed to keep the world from slipping into chaos.

Care for the Deceased and the Phenomenon of Natural Dehydration

One of the unique discoveries made possible by the very hot and dry climate of the Egyptian desert bordering the Nile Valley was the potential to dehydrate and preserve a human body long after that person was deceased. In what were probably accidental and unintended discoveries of human bodies in the dry sands of the desert, it was quite noticeable that the body was in very much the same condition as it had appeared while alive. Most noticeable, perhaps was the person's hair, which showed little or no evidence of change. If braided, it was still braided. If wavy, it was still wavy. Clothing likewise tended to remain intact. Skin tone and color, although taking on a leathery appearance, were likely very much the same over a skeletal frame that had not changed at all. Decomposition, in other words, seemed to be suspended. It was as if the deceased person had transcended life with essentially the same body but existed in a different world unfettered by the stresses and strains of the contemporary world.

Royal Immortality

It was a small leap of the imagination to visualize that whole person existing in an alternative or subterranean world filled with all of the positives that living in Egypt could provide an eternity of blissful paradise. The individuals most likely to visualize the importance of transcending from anonymity to everlasting life in a blissful state would be the early members of the priesthood and ranking members of the nobility intent upon honoring the highest levels of the royal family. As with much early formation of mythology, the imagination dwells on the positive aspects of how it might be to exist for eternity in paradise free from all the risk factors that dominate the lives of even the most exalted families. The message was so strong, in fact, that early royal families of ancient Egyptian cultures started the process of preparing for the royal's everlasting life from the beginning of their reign until the actual time of their death. The early mastabas (rectangular tombs and predecessors of the pyramid) were built to contain rooms much like those the royals occupied during their life with food, drink, furniture, objects of art, war, and symbols of power that would accompany the royals in the afterlife. Royals would be raised from early childhood to be fully convinced that their life would be extraordinary both in the present and the perpetual afterlife that would be even more fulfilling. Tombs became more and more embellished, leading to the construction of Khufu's Great Pyramid of Giza with 2.3 million blocks, secret chambers, and superhuman efforts to create immortal monuments and chambers filled with treasures and artistic representations of their life's accomplishments. One of the problems with such ostentatiousness, however, was the coordinated teams of tomb robbers that simultaneously created secret accesses to the tomb of priceless treasures, or did so later due to the extremely obvious location within a monumental pyramid. Thus, for a 400-year period of time, there was a real effort to make royal tombs more clandestine in the mountainous Valley of the Kings. The issue of tomb robbers showing their contempt for their pharaoh's struggle to ascend into the afterlife was a concern during real time as one royal family was replaced by another, yet the concept of everlasting life was far too pervasive and too difficult to deny to diminish the validity of an altruistic and euphoric life after death for their royal and possibly divine leadership. The more jaundiced members of ancient Egyptian society, not unlike other societies since that time, contained a diverse mix of unsavory, greedy, and ruthless people throughout the economic hierarchy who were willing to risk death to share in the riches of the deceased pharaoh's tomb. The fact that such robberies were a transgression against the gods failed to be a deterrent.

Expansion of Immortality

A side issue of the divine right of royals to an everlasting life of harmonious euphoria may have been the recognition that both endeared and detested pharaohs could expect a life after death that was totally satisfying to them in spite of their behavior when alive. It was therefore just a small step for other significant members of the royal family who arrived there by whatever means and powerful members of the priesthood who were privy to the trivial and ordinary ins and outs of the royal family to want the same reward for themselves. Because of the inability to disprove the existence of the afterlife that had consumed so much of the focus of Egyptian royal life, it was inevitable that ranking members of the priesthood as well as affluent citizens at large would seek a comparable life of bliss after death. The lesser tombs that continue to be discovered throughout Egypt are evidence of the sweeping importance of an irrefutable desire to be included in a perpetual paradise after death and apart from the masses. The blissful notion of a perpetual afterlife, however, was seriously complicated by the intrusions of hundreds of different Egyptian gods and goddesses who had their own quirky behaviors and potential to interfere with the process of attaining everlasting life.

Early Evolution of the Afterlife

Evidence discovered in some of the earliest tombs of royal families illustrates the early belief in and emphasis on all of the attributes of a perpetual and euphoric afterlife in an environment such as that experienced within the Nile Valley. One of the first transitions from burial in a vast wasteland of desert that soon becomes covered over by shifting sands was elementary stages of mummification to remove the fluids and soft tissues of the body, perhaps treat the body with salt crystals or other drying agents, and to wrap the body with linen and keep it in a protected and dry place. The Egyptian fascination with death became a progressively more ritualized transition from one royal family to the next. The mummification process was intended to be in tune with the multitude of gods and goddesses that had evolved, and the central focus of that preparation was the ascent into the afterlife. The process began early in the reign of the new king (pharaoh) and was carefully monitored throughout his reign. Glorifying the process to be anticipated after death was a means of communicating with the deities who would help to protect the Egyptian people and to ensure the successful reign of their king. By the time of Seti I, father of Rameses II, the king declared himself for the first time to be an actual deity during his reign, not after completing the twelve stages of passage into the afterlife that were to be completed within the first twelve months after death. Rameses II furthered the deification process during a 67-year reign (1279-1213 BCE) by portraying himself as a living deity on a scale with the most important gods and even extended divinity to his wife, Nefertari. Among his many notorious accomplishments was a record of having approximately 162 children by his principal wives and consorts. Among the many distinct sculpted images that he left for posterity were the much bigger-than-life sculptures of himself, his wife, Nefertari, and principal gods seated together at Abu Simbel near the southern border of Egypt.

Ramesses II

2
The Origins of Regional Monotheism
The Enigmas of Abraham (Abram)

One of the many enigmas of the founding father of three of the world's great religions is that Abraham was considered a charismatic, powerful military leader and religious independent who may have been from a Northern Mesopotamian township of Ur, not the Sumerian/Babylonian city of Ur that was later known as Ur of Chaldea. In the Old Testament descriptions, he was never considered a gullible tribesman and herder of sheep who periodically heard the voice of God. This historically unique personage, who was the fountainhead of three great faiths, might have been invented if he had not actually existed. He exists in the legends and folklore of the people who believe in him and he represents antiquity's early confrontation with the crossroads of paganism and belief in one true living God.

There continues to be debate in reference to Abraham's actual birthplace and early influences. He may or may not have been exposed to the thriving city of Ur near the Mesopotamian capital of Babylon, around the time period of 2,000 BCE. That particular city existed at a very prosperous time within the "cradle of civilization" region of the Middle East (now southern Iraq) and was notable for having a huge, tiered pyramid known as a ziggurat. However, assuming that Abraham was born into a minority culture of Semitic-language people within the dominant Babylonian/Sumerian culture, he would have been raised alongside a pagan culture that had long expressed hostilities toward Semitic culture people living to the west of them. He likely spoke either Akkadian or Aramaic, as written evidence of Old Hebrew has not been found prior to about 1,000 BCE. Instead of being a simple herder of sheep and cattle who mentally wrestled with conflicts between pagan deities and the one true god, he was also a fortune-hunting adventurer and successful military leader. In one particular battle against Mesopotamian forces, it is recorded that Abraham divided his numerically inferior force of men armed with sickle swords, six-foot long spears and shields, and made an unconventional night attack from several different directions. His commando-like forces utilized surprise, stealth, flaming torches, and loud noises to overwhelm and slaughter his intended enemies and to rescue his nephew, Lot.

As an adult, Abraham traveled westward from the city of Ur to the city of Haran. Soon, during a time of drought and famine, his faith in God and the Promised Land was severely challenged and he relocated to Egypt with his nephew, Lot. It is noted (Genesis 13 1-2) that Abraham became very rich in cattle, silver, and gold during his sojourn in southern Egypt. It was also noted (Genesis 16 3) that Abraham's wife, Sarah, was barren and therefore gave her Egyptian servant, Hagar, to him to be his additional wife. Eventually, he had a son by his second wife named Ishmael. Among the consequences of the multiple-wife relationship were major strife and jealousy within the patriarchal family and Ishmael's eventual expulsion from Abraham's tent (Genesis 21 8-14). Extended periods of strife between Abraham and Lot take on a metaphoric quality of contrasting pure and almost divine motives, generosity, and sacrifices with Lot's desire for self-interest and unlimited wealth. The object lesson portrayed is that Lot compares unfavorably with Abraham in nearly every respect. Finally, Lot is described as the last moral individual in the debauched cities of Sodom and Gomorrah. He is visited by two angels, and rather than allow those angels to be debauched by the local citizenry, he agrees to evacuate the morally decadent city with his family but must promise to not look back. Of course, as might be predicted, Lot's wife does look back (Genesis 19 26) and all of his possessions were destroyed and his wife was turned into a pillar of salt. Abraham, in contrast, is viewed as the patriarch, the one who rebelled against pagan gods, who believed in a living god, and who would become known as the "father of nations." Abraham is the devout believer who allowed his faith to be tested by the living god when he accepted God's command to offer up his son in sacrifice, but just as he was about to do so with great anguish, was allowed to substitute a goat for the ritual sacrifice.

Hebrew or Mitanni Migrants

3
Babylon and Canaan at the Time of Abraham
Linguistic and Pagan Migrations

One of the major keys to identifying ethnic origins in both time and place is to consider the evolution of the spoken and written word for particular groups of people. The Chaldeans were an early group of Semitic people centered near the northern end of the Persian Gulf who co-existed with Arameans and Shutu peoples of the region that would later be known as Babylon. Ultimately the Chaldeans were absorbed into the dominant Babylonian culture and acquired major elements of the Akkadian language. During the late Assyrian Empire Period, however, the Akkadian/Babylonian language fell out of favor and was replaced by Aramaic throughout much of Mesopotamia. This now rarely spoken language was once regarded as the lingua franca of the Middle East and was the primary language of the people in Palestine at the time of Jesus. The Hebrew language was common to the region now known as Israel and emerged about 1,000 BCE within the Canaanite family of languages. That family of languages includes Hebrew, Ammonite, and Moabite (Jordanian) in the southern Canaanite region, while the Phoenician language is associated with the northern and western Canaanite region nearer to present-day Lebanon. Some Canaanite languages and dialects have become extinct. Aramaic, however, being a regional language of trade, became a principal language of the Babylonian people, which was also influenced by southern and central Arabic. The Hebrew language, however, was a well-established spoken language in the Canaan region from at least the tenth century BCE until it died down due to the Babylonian invasion of Canaan in 586 BCE. Major numbers of affluent, Hebrew-speaking people were deported to that Mesopotamian Empire hundreds of miles to the east for a period of approximately 70 years and acquired a facility for Aramaic, the language of their captors. In possessing great facility with languages, they retained Hebrew as the language of their religion and sacred writings.

Hebrew, like Aramaic, is a Semitic language derived from the Afro-Asiatic, i.e., Mid-Eastern family of languages. Presently it is spoken and written by more than seven million people in the State of Israel where both Hebrew and Arabic are official languages. Linguistically, the Samaritans are descended from the same Israelite stock as the rest of the Israelites and continue to use Biblical Hebrew as their liturgical language as do many of the Jewish people. The Samaritans were a religious group who claimed their worship was the true religion of the ancient Israelites prior to the Babylonian Exile. Their beliefs were preserved by the people who remained in the Land of Israel, as opposed to Judaism, which they assert is a related but altered and amended religion brought back by the exiled returnees. Therefore, in the New Testament, Samaria is viewed negatively as the home of this non-orthodox group.

The earliest written evidence of the Hebrew language dates back to the Gezer Calendar around the tenth century BCE. The style of the language at that time has been classified as Old or Archaic Hebrew. The language was written in an old Semitic script similar to a Phoenician style that evolved through the Greeks and Etruscans to later become Roman script. The Old Hebrew script has some resemblance to Egyptian hieroglyphs but tended to follow different rules of grammar such as omitting vowels and being far less pictographic. This Old or Archaic version of Hebrew using Canaanite script was extant from the tenth century BCE, and likely earlier times, until the Babylonian Exile in the sixth century BCE. During that 70-year period of captivity the language evolved into Classical or Biblical Hebrew, utilized in the formation of early books of the Old Testament. Aramaic, the language that Jesus Christ spoke, was widespread in the northern and eastern regions of the Middle East. It was one of the relatively universal languages of the region and originally the language of the desert-dwelling Aramaean people. For many Hebrews, however, the Aramaic language was resented and represented the detested period of Babylonian captivity. This ancient language, in its many variations or dialects, was far more than the language of Jesus Christ. It is considered to be an endangered language today, yet it has a long history as a distinct language group within the Middle East. However, the severity of dialectic variations has directly contributed to Aramaic's demise. The once quite sacred and secular language has definite Semitic origins but is something of a subgroup of the more dominant languages within that broad region. It is included within the Canaanite family of languages, such as Hebrew, but also bears some relationship to Arabic. Aramaic was used in much of the early Talmud and fluency in that language might contribute to a clearer understanding of the actual words of Jesus Christ. There are still people who speak Aramaic, such as some Syrian Christians, and people who study the language, but the pitfalls of translation from one language to another are apparent and subject to being out of context from the original intent. Only a few fragments of the New Testament that were written in Aramaic have survived. A few scholars have speculated that the original language of the authors of the gospels of Matthew and Mark was Aramaic because of peculiarities in the original Greek. If there ever was an original gospel written in Aramaic, it has not survived. Following the 70-year capture of the prominent Israelites by the Babylonians in 586-516 BCE, the Hebrew speakers who resettled in their homeland cast aspersions on Aramaic as the resented language of their captors. Currently Hebrew and Arabic are the official languages of Israel, not Aramaic. Few Christians appear to make an effort to learn Aramaic yet, due to the powers of divinity, fully anticipate being able to communicate with Christ in their own language.

The Phoenician language was concentrated along the western coastal regions especially in the northern section of ancient Canaan and modern Lebanon. The Phoenician people were noted for being a resourceful maritime trading culture with frequent contact with other eastern Mediterranean people such as the Canaanites, Egyptians, Minoans, Greeks, Assyrians, Hittites, and others in the region possibly as far as Spain and cities along the northern coast of Africa. The city of Tyre appears to have marked their southern boundary. The Phoenician language was descended from Canaanite and is also considered a Semitic language. One of the cultural distinctions, apart from language, was that the worldly Phoenician people did not practice male circumcision as was common for most Semitic people. Little is certain about the origins of the Phoenician people except to acknowledge that there was a long history of intermingling with Canaanite and other indigenous people. The territory occupied by the Phoenicians along the coastline of the eastern Mediterranean has been a well-traveled crossroad for nomadic peoples since the earliest of times.

4
Egypt Around the Time Period of 1600 BCE

The ancient world's most accomplished and diversified civilization had been established and evolving for approximately 2,000 years by the year 1600 BCE. The authoritarian and pharaoh-driven Old Kingdom that culminated with the construction of the grand pyramids on the Giza Plateau had existed for several millennia of continuous Egyptian history. The Middle Kingdom (2040-1640 BCE) experienced many transformations due to both internal and external pressures. It was a time of declining competence of the weakened monarchies and bloated priesthood intent on acquiring wealth, knowledge, and power. New classes of artisans, builders, traders, military officers, merchants, and farmers were becoming more conscious of their collective power and rights as the top-heavy bureaucracy of government, military, and priesthood made increasing demands on the citizenry. The failings of weaker pharaohs (kings) who showed their insecurities as war leaders and as financial administrators during difficult times emboldened the populace and external enemies as well.

The Egyptian World of Paganism and Obsession with Immortality

The subdivisions of ancient Egypt vied for increasing shares of local power and revenue. The complex religious structure that could be interpreted in different ways in the different regions placed increased reliance upon its local gods and goddesses for divine deliverance. The funerary rituals, sacrifices, and beliefs that had once been confined to the very highest levels of the royal family and elite members of the priesthood began to spread among the more affluent and powerful classes that were emerging. No longer was the royal privilege of a blessed immortality in the afterlife limited to the pharaoh, his family, and select high priests. The growth of upper classes outside of government and religion was evidenced by the desires of the wealthy to have well-furnished tombs and embalming suitable for the afterlife. The all-powerful royal funerary god, Osiris, gradually became accessible to all who had the means for ritualized funerals and the promise of a perpetual life after death within the paradise of Egypt. Many such grave sites have since been discovered, confirming the expanding desire among the affluent masses to have an idealized life after death. After all, there was no means to effectively challenge the validity of such a future existence. The uniquely creative Egyptian approach was to enunciate an arduous number of twelve steps and challenges that had to be met within the first twelve months after death to reach that euphoric and perpetual post-life of bliss. The affluent and elite could pay to be buried in mastabas and rock-cut tombs that would be decorated in stylistic and graphic ways to demonstrate and confirm their belief that an idealized afterlife was attainable. The magic appeal of a euphoric life after death, although such a life is not provable, has captured the human imagination for at least the past four millennia.

Ancient Egypt Prior to Moses

During this period, a period of steady decline within the Thirteenth Dynasty, northern Egypt, in particular, continued to lose much of its former power and cohesion. The military leaders located near the southern border of Egypt tended to affiliate themselves more and more with the former rival population in

Nubia and became more and more independent of the central authority of Thebes. Fortifications along the eastern border to protect against incursions by Libyan adventurers tended to be abandoned or increasingly neglected. Canaanite nomads immigrated into the Northern Delta region with increasing numbers and with little resistance. Their numbers increased to such an extent that one of their numbers, Khendjer, was able to declare himself a king. By the end of the Thirteenth Dynasty, the eastern delta of the Nile Valley was populated mostly by Middle Easterners of Semitic origin. Descendants of these same people would represent a preponderance of the ethnically non-Egyptian residents of the Delta region that Moses would ultimately lead out of Egypt. Prior to the Exodus there were centuries of what might be considered minority laborer status and perhaps even indentured laborer status, but not slave laborer status except for possibly captured enemies. These Semitic people of Canaanite origin with their own distinctive religious and cultural beliefs were the people that Moses led out of Egypt following the great plagues and supernatural events that paved the way. From the Egyptian point of view, the steadily increasing numbers of Canaanite people who staunchly refused to assimilate into the theocracy of Egypt represented an increasing threat of rising against the (Hyksos) pharaoh's failing government. The Egyptian response had been to make continued residency for the Canaanite people as difficult as possible without losing control over them. The Egyptian government during this same, poorly documented period, was of Semitic origin (possibly a subgroup of Canaan, Assyria, Amorite, Hittite, or Mesopotamian origin), but tried to accept the Egyptian deities in addition to their own, compared to the ethnic subgroup in the Delta that staunchly accepted monotheism only.

Semitic (Hyksos) Occupation of Lower Egypt
Fifteenth and Sixteenth Dynasties, circa 1684-1567 BCE
The Hyksos, a militarily powerful group of Semitic people to the northeast of Egypt, had been drifting toward or encroaching upon their southern neighbor by assimilation for many generations, and then invaded by force in approximately 1650 BCE. They had adapted to the Egyptian language and culture sufficiently to recognize the weaknesses of the old monarchy in the northern half of Egypt and were able to impose their own hybrid form of government and control of the region for approximately 80 years. Their expulsion appears to be synonymous with the story of Moses and the Exodus, but that depends on which source is telling the story.

The political situation in Egypt during that period was riddled with internal and external problems. Lower Egypt (that is, the northern half) in particular was becoming saturated with immigrants and possibly invading swarms of people known to the Egyptians as the Hyksos, or "shepherd kings," who set up two different dynasties. The occupation by these "foreign Hyksos invaders" with superior composite, recurved bows, and superior fast-moving, horse-drawn war chariots was at a time of Egyptian complacency and internal weakness, and was limited to Lower (northern) Egypt. The invasion by these non-Egyptian, Semitic people who lived for centuries to the immediate north and northeast of the Egyptian Delta was likely accomplished more by open migration and quasi-settlement in the region for extended periods of time than by a massive assault by the far better armed and equipped northern invaders. Egyptian resistance was ineffectual due to inferior military tactics, equipment, and due to political and financial weaknesses at the time. The Hyksos people had interacted with the Delta people for such extended periods that they were increasingly absorbed into the dominant Egyptian culture. Hyskos rulers accepted Egyptian titles as their own and adopted the Egyptian god, Seth (the dog god) as one of their principal deities. Evidence is good that these occupying masses with many of their own beliefs and cultural traditions were tolerated by the people of northern Egypt but continued to be viewed as intruders who would never be allowed to fully assimilate into the dominant Egyptian culture. The Hyksos people, a distinct Semitic minority from both Canaan and Syria, set up their new capital in Northern Egypt and named it Avaris. The people of Upper (southern) Egypt continued to worship the god Horus as their primary god for protection. Ultimately, after approximately eighty years of Hyksos rule, resentment boiled over, the Egyptian military finally adapted to new ways, and the Hyksos were driven out of Egypt. The native Egyptian rulers of the Eighteenth Dynasty (direct descendants of the Seventeenth Dynasty of Thebes) took control and did all within their power to erase the influence of the Hyksos. The victors within their own traditional lands for many thousands of years could write their history from their own point of view and diminish or exclude the significance of the Hyksos occupation period and the impact of different but related Semitic people who left the Delta region as one big colony in a successful grand exodus. The southern portion of Egypt (Upper because it is up river on the Nile) was never occupied by the Hyksos people and continued to be governed by recognized kings (pharaoh was not a term used in ancient times) based at the capital of Thebes until the invaders were eventually ousted.

The Fifteenth Dynasty (1674-1567 BCE) had a succession of Hyksos kings, and the Sixteenth Dynasty (1684-1567 BCE) was notable for a number of vassal chiefs who conceded more and more to pressures from the dominant Egyptian population. Early kings with Canaanite names included Sakir-Har (name found etched into stone at Avaris), Khyan, c. 1620 BCE; Apophis, c. 1580 to 1540 BCE; and Khamudi, c. 1540 to 1534 BCE. These border-crossers from the north were definitely Semitic people who originated just outside of ancient Egypt and were probably of Canaanite, Amorite, and Syrian (Assyrian) origin. In addition to language, cultural, and religious cohesiveness, one of the distinguishing features of the Semitic people was ritualized circumcision of infant males which was practiced without exception. Oddly, there is evidence in the ancient Egyptian record of royals being publicly circumcised as young men rather than as infants as evidenced in the tomb of Ankh-ma-hor at Saqqara.

Hyksos Expulsion from Lower Egypt Simultaneous with Exodus

Once the Hyksos invaders were ousted by the Egyptians from the south, after a period of approximately 80 years, great efforts were made to erase nearly every trace of their existence. As a consequence, the Old Testament, written in stages centuries after that time, could only identify the ruler of Egypt at the time of the Exodus as "pharaoh," not by a specific name. As will be shown later, the Exodus can be reliably pinpointed to a range of 25 years before or after 1600 BCE on the basis of firm geologic data. The apparent absence of acknowledgement of an event in Egyptian history as great as the Exodus and the impact of the ten great plagues associated with that event is more readily understandable. Oral traditions certainly kept such a major historical/biblical event alive among the Hebrew people with little emphasis on the specific king of the Nile Delta area of Lower Egypt at the time. The Hyksos pharaoh who capitulated to the demands of the very large, expanding, and restive minority of Semitic

Hebrews who occupied the eastern Nile Delta would have been the obscure king Sakir-Har, or king Khyan. Upper Egypt (in the south) would have been impacted little by the Exodus so far to the north during a time period that was not favorable for Egyptian unity or historical pride. The dramatic scale of the Exodus event for the Hebrew minority who exited from Egypt as an entire colony and the reinforcement of their unique, monotheistic faith was a world-altering event. Oral traditions would very much sustain the major elements of that complex event as the storytellers kept the details alive to the best of their understanding. For the Egyptians, it was the expulsion of the Semitic Hyksos. For the Israelites, the same event was the Exodus.

The expulsion of the Semitic Hyksos people by the re-grouped forces of Upper (southern) Egypt is almost certain to be one simultaneous event with the Exodus from the Egyptian point of view. For the Egyptian authorities, it made far more sense to emphasize the defeat and ejection of the Hyksos people than to acknowledge being bamboozled by thousands of alien resident laborers in the region of Goshen. Philosophically and militarily outmaneuvering and outwitting the king of Upper Egypt (or possibly the Hyksos king) would forever be a world-class accomplishment. Geologic conditions of epic proportions coincided with the collision of Hebrew resentment of being treated as a despised minority worker population when the real concern of the weak Hyksos government was fear that the growing numbers and strength of the Hebrew minority in their midst threatened to topple the fading "shepherd king" claim to control of Lower Egypt. Ironically, some parallel circumstances almost 400 years later during the long and powerful reign of Rameses II have led a few researchers to believe the Exodus may have occurred about 1250 BCE, but the evidence is not sufficient. Also, directives to

Imaginary Exodus scene

the scribes of the Old Testament tended to stretch lifespans, such as Moses dying at the mythological age of 120 years (Deuteronomy 347), saying hundreds of thousands of people wondered the desert for 40 years, or averaging the Exodus generations at 40 years instead of a much more typical 20-25 years, must have been intended to make historical and biblical events more readily coincide. A realistic account of the Exodus (and simultaneous expulsion of the Hyksos) could have been an equally dramatic story without the hyperbole of myth-making.

5
Egyptian Exodus Mystery

The most provocative mystery regarding the Exodus, an integral element of Hebrew religion, history, and culture, is the precise date within a few decades to either side of such a monumental and world-changing event, not a discrepancy of a few centuries. The written records to be found in otherwise thorough Egyptian histories have been largely mute on the subject. The actual name of the reigning pharaoh during this earth-shaking, watershed moment in the history of the Jewish people has never been recorded in the Old Testament, or other source. This is especially difficult to understand since it was an open challenge and public defeat of the pharaoh's authority and military power. The reasons for such a gross omission on the part of an Egyptian monarchy may have been the tendency to not record military defeats; especially the embarrassing failure to return maybe 5,000 to 10,000 poorly armed and poorly trained men, women, and children to the Goshen territory as ordered by the pharaoh. One possible explanation is that the Israelite exodus was an embarrassment to Egypt and the sudden loss of a large work force precipitated the defeat of the Hyksos invaders who had been in power for just over 100 years. The ousting of the Hyksos government was followed by rigorous efforts to destroy all trace of their resented presence and to restore order in a vast region that was obsessed with the avoidance of chaos. Authors of the Old Testament, beginning many centuries after the fact, likely could no longer recall what amounted to an insignificant name of the last or next-to-last Hyksos ruler when Moses led his large contingent of disgruntled and harassed minority workers and their families out of Egypt.

Various coincidences with the brief reign and heretical beliefs of the pharaoh, Akhenaten (1378-1361 BCE) have been associated with the time period of the Exodus. The most important coincidence relates to Akhenaten being the only king of ancient Egypt to believe in a single god. It has been argued by Ahmed Osman, in his book, *Moses and Akhenaten*, that Akhenaten escaped assassination by literally becoming Moses. That assumption appears to be invalidated by the recent study published in the Journal of the American Medical Association (volume 303, Number 7, February 17, 2010) that states in part, "Genetic fingerprinting allowed the construction of a 5-generation pedigree of Tutankhamun's immediate lineage. The KV55 mummy and KV35YL were identified as the parents of Tutankhamun." The historical record had not previously documented the death of Akhenaten, but it has been known for some time that KV55 appeared to be a hastily constructed "dumping ground" for relics associated with the "heretic" Amarna king

An alternate hypothesis with less credibility was that the very powerful pharaoh, Rameses II, who ruled well after Akhenaten, was the pharaoh at the time of Moses. A third assumption was that Adikam, a pharaoh who ruled for only four years prior to drowning in the Red (Reed?) Sea, was a successor to Malul, a pharaoh who ruled from the age of six to the age of 100 years. Another possible candidate for pharaoh with an extremely long reign at the time of the Exodus was Pepi II of the Sixth Dynasty. His was the last dynasty of the Old Kingdom in Egypt. It is totally improbable that Moses could have been the chagrined Akhenaten, Egypt's first and only monotheistic pharaoh for 17 years, who was unceremoniously dethroned and probably assassinated. Another speculation with some merit is that Ahmoses was the pharaoh at the time of the Exodus because of similarities with the name "Moses," and other factors.

Mystery of the Unnamed Pharaoh

There is some historical evidence for the (unnamed) pharaoh's growing concern with the rapidly increasing population of Goshen by people whose adamant religious beliefs clashed sharply with Egyptian religion and who might be a threat to the Egyptian government. These immigrant workers had been peacefully settling into the eastern delta region of the Nile for many centuries. They are believed to be people from the Canaanite region just to the north who fiercely clung to their own religious beliefs rather than assimilate into the Egyptian culture. The cohesiveness and stubbornness of this large foreign minority within the northeast border of Egypt did have the potential to represent a destabilizing influence. Historical records do show that repressive measures were implemented to stifle continued growth of a potentially hostile minority within Egypt's northeastern borders. The consequences of repressive measures were likely to be threatening to both sides. It was not a rampant situation of masters and slaves except for possible war captives or as a punishment for criminal behavior. To the Egyptians, the lands of Canaan and Assyria (later Syria and Lebanon) were just buffer regions to protect themselves from sudden attack by the Hittite super-powers in Anatolia (most of current Turkey) to the north and Mesopotamian powers to the northeast.

The Essence of the Story of Moses

The story of Moses has been told over and over for approximately 3,600 years without significant change to the basic details. The story of pharaonic abuse of power by ordering all Jewish male infants to be slain due to rapid population increase is subject to debate. Such stories have literary parallels in the Gilgamesh epic and the mandate of Herod at the time of Christ's birth. Also, the story of the infant Moses being found by the pharaoh's daughter in a basket floating down the Nile runs parallel with ancient stories of important personages surviving in the same manner and going on to accomplish great things. For one thing, a pharaoh's daughter was not likely to be unaccompanied at the river's edge, and even more dicey issues of royal parentage and royal marriageability would be raised if a single daughter claimed to be the mother of an infant. The conventional story is that the infant Moses was raised within the royal family and wet-nursed by his actual mother. As a young adult prince within the unnamed royal family, Moses suddenly felt a kinship with, and empathized with, a Jewish worker who was being abused by an Egyptian overseer. He struck the overseer and the man died. As a result, Moses needed to leave Egypt to avoid being ostracized by the royal family and perhaps charged with murder. An interval of time elapsed and Moses returned to the large Jewish population centered in the Goshen area of northeast Egypt. He and his brother, Aaron, were able to communicate with the royal family as the pharaoh was confronted with one severe plague after another and finally relented and granted the Jewish request to return to their original homeland to the northeast. As anticipated, however, the pharaoh reneged on his promise and sent the Egyptian army complete with infantry, archers, and armed chariot drivers to return this rebellious population of possibly 5,000 to 10,000 disenchanted workers and their families to the region known as Goshen. The Bible describes the Hebrews in Egypt as having only two midwives. That number suggests that the Hebrew population in Goshen at the time of Moses was in the thousands, not hundreds of thousands.

The Israelite people of Goshen reportedly anticipated resistance to their plan to relocate the entire colony and had been amassing weapons and food supplies by whatever means, including theft, in violation of Egyptian laws. The true brilliance of Moses is revealed in his organizing a potentially lethal relocation plan, his reconnoitering of routes that would neutralize a hot pursuit by the pharaoh's armed troops, and navigating treacherous routes in an unforgiving territory of mountains and desert through a completely indirect route to the Promised Land of Canaan. Some scholars consider the Exodus saga to be a fabricated merger of actual mass migrations due to economic, geologic, and political factors.

Exodus of Oppressed Minority Workers, Not Slaves

The mass evacuation of a very large community of Jewish workers, their families, all of their possessions plus food, water, and assorted weapons amounts to a superhuman effort. The only means of transport were makeshift wagons, some beasts of burden, and their own backs. Food and water to sustain very large numbers of people in a desert wilderness would alone produce more bulk weight than the typical adult in good health could manage. One parallel, however, did occur in 1877 when one-armed General Oliver Otis Howard was directed by President Grant to order the Nez Perce people onto an Oklahoma reservation from the pristine mountains of eastern Oregon, or be declared hostile and subject to imprisonment or death. The Nez Perce tribes gathered their possessions and herded their cattle and horses across swollen, spring run-off rivers and some of the steepest mountain wilderness in North America, and fended off four U.S. army assaults before surrendering to General Nelson Miles just a few miles south of the Canadian border. The exhausted Nez Perce people of all ages camped briefly outside of Canada and were surrounded by Gen. Miles' army only because of the superior ability of the telegraph to communicate the exact location of the Nez Perce. The physical needs and capabilities of the human body have not changed in any appreciable way in the past 3,600 years. The potential for "living off the land" in a barren wilderness likewise will not sustain hundreds of thousands of people of all ages for any length of time, and certainly not for forty years. The comment about roaming the wilderness for a period of forty years can only be taken as a metaphor for an extremely arduous journey, not a physiological reality. One story after another of miraculous extraction of water from rocks and nutrition from thin air reads more like a storyteller's device and detracts from the actual sacrifices made. Large flocks of sheep could be a source of sustenance, but what will sustain large herds of sheep, cattle, horses, and donkeys?

The consequences for the weak and humiliated government of Egypt after the Exodus are likewise difficult to pinpoint but were marked with invasions by historic rivals such as the Nubian/Ethiopian people at the southern border, Libyan tribesmen to the east and Hittite, Canaanite, or Amorite pressures from the north and northeast. The kings of Egypt during the period of chaos that followed Exodus were mostly of Ethiopian, Libyan, or Mid-Eastern descent. Moses, who may have been a member of the pharaonic court at one time, was reported to have married a Midianite woman, not an Ethiopian woman as recorded by some sources. The Midianites were part of an Arabian tribe who principally inhabited the desert north of the peninsula of Arabia. Other developments around the time of the Middle Kingdom of Egypt were the decline of the Bronze Age and the introduction of better-quality edged weapons with the introduction of the Iron Age. It was during the Late Bronze Age that the Canaanite people spoke and wrote in what is now called Biblical Hebrew.

Further, it was considered to be around the end of the Bronze Age that Canaanite cities such as Jericho, Ai, and Arad were destroyed by the Israelites. Significant gaps exist in the multiple invasions and resettlements of the Canaanite territories over a period of many hundreds of years. Cultural assimilation with the Israelites coming back from the southern region (Egypt) and the dominant, Hebrew-speaking Canaanites, Assyrians, and other tribes from the north and east appear to have melded into fiercely independent followers of Abraham, Isaac, Jacob, and Moses. Another historical point of reference is that Joshua, the military successor of Moses, selected the very ancient city of Jericho to the north of the Dead Sea and near the ancient city of Jerusalem as the first city of Canaan to utterly destroy. The Israelite campaign to take control of all of Canaan was reported to have consumed a period of over 400 years.

The Military Brilliance of Moses

Moses, like his successor, Joshua, may be looked upon as a brilliant military strategist, among his other attributes. The successful evacuation of the Israelites was a world-altering accomplishment that required great planning, preparation, cunning, fortuitous timing, and physical execution virtually unmatched in the history of the world. Planning an escape route required the brilliance of knowing about the changing, marshy conditions of the Reed Sea (not the infinitely larger Red Sea) and getting large numbers of people and animals through that labyrinth at a fast walking pace and in advance of an Egyptian army bent on their destruction. A combination of seasonal factors including a strong east wind, low tides, and a carefully selected and marked route could explain their success and the failure of a chariot-dependent army led by an angry pharaoh into what amounted to a watery, marshy trap.

To ensure the trap, Moses would have instructed others to maintain a smoking pillar (a portable fire of great size with a metal hood will produce a pillar of smoke) during the day. The same portable fire during the night without a hood would appear at a distance to be a pillar of fire and give the impression that the Israelites were moving in a large circle that would lead to their entrapment, but in reality was ensuring that the Egyptian army was moving into a watery trap that would mark their doom. Finally, Moses turned south along the Sinai Peninsula instead of the direct northern route to Canaan because it was known that Egyptian military were stationed in the area now known as Gaza and would have been in a position to intercept and destroy a poorly equipped and poorly trained mass of refugees. The initial successes were soon followed by dissension and a tendency to revert to pagan beliefs during Moses' ascent of Mt. Sinai for the revealed purpose of communicating with the Hebrew god and to impose a codified set of laws in the form of the Ten Commandments. The story of Moses' wrath when he returns with the stone tablets to see people practicing idolatry is to throw the divinely inscribed tablets down the mountain, smashing them into bits. Later, the story is retold to indicate that a second set of commandments were produced and placed within an Ark of the Covenant that possessed mystic powers and continues to be lost to this date. The story tends to get caught up in rivalries and physical sacrifices that nearly doom the expedition to the promised land of Canaan and ends with an exaggerated lifespan for Moses of 120 years. Also, God prohibited Moses from entering Canaan due to a showy miracle of tapping a rod on a stone three times to get water when God, who conversed with him earlier, had instructed him to perform the miracle in a different way. The search for the mysterious Mt. Sinai of Moses has been narrowed to at least eight possible sites, and presently the unfulfilled quest of over 3,400 years may be narrowed down to a Saudi Arabian site called Jebel el-Lawz that is blocked off from further search by the Saudi Arabian government. The quest for Moses and the lost Ark of the Covenant continues to be an insatiable goal for true believers.

During an extended period of ancient Egyptian complacency toward the outside world, chariot design and military tactics of the Semitic Hyksos people improved sufficiently to overcome the Egyptian army of Lower Egypt (northern Egypt). The Hyksos occupiers were driven out of northeastern Egypt about 80 years later following the Egyptian armies' technological improvements of the chariot. Centuries later, in the time of Ramesses II, chariot design again had to be improved to compete with the heavier chariots of their Hittite rivals.

6
The Ten Plagues of Egypt

Super-Extraordinary Events Associated with the Exodus
Blood-red water suddenly appeared in all open bodies of water including ponds, streams, canals, water containers, and even the (Lower) Nile. Soon any fish in those waters died and floated on the surface or decayed on the banks.

Infestation of frogs was so severe that land near bodies of water was saturated with them and frogs were found inside people's homes. Hordes of small flying insects such as gnats, small flies, and fruit flies saturated the air and tormented animals and people alike. Hordes of black flies filled the air and spread infectious diseases.

Livestock diseases became rampant and infected domesticated animals such as cattle, sheep, goats, horses, camels, and donkeys. Infectious boils appeared on animals and people alike throughout the area. Dirty hail storms pelted everything in the open and destroyed standing crops. The hailstones were sometimes large enough to cause fatal injuries. Swarms of locusts (a relative of the grasshopper) appeared and consumed all vegetation that survived the hailstorm.

Events That May Have Preceded the Exodus

Historically, it was the final plague incident that was the most effective disaster in compelling the reigning pharaoh to yield to the pleas of Moses and his brother, Aaron, to "let my people go!" It can be readily imagined that shocking plagues and tragic events were sufficient to produce a great panic among the populace. The events, coming one right after another, would have been too severe and too bizarre for the affected people to accept as natural events. Considering the superstitions and reliance on a broad range of gods, there may have been the appearance of an open power struggle between the gods of Egypt and the one true god of the Israelites. Animosities between the Semitic resident aliens in Goshen and the Egyptian authorities had been intensifying for years as the alien population grew and represented a political threat to a potentially weak government of the Lower Nile. The Exodus may have been opportunistic given the exceedingly unusual and terrifying circumstances, but the successful evacuation of possibly tens of thousands of people of all ages required advance planning and leadership. Small numbers of Semitic laborers and their families could probably cross the Egyptian border at will and for that reason were far more likely to be minority laborers, not slaves. There was evidence that the growing size of this reluctant-to-assimilate minority was seen as a threat by the royal authorities and systematic pressures were being placed to limit the power of this intruder population. Given the apparent power of the Hebrew god over the Egyptian gods, the infamous, unnamed pharaoh granted permission for the entire colony to leave Egypt. However, it was soon recognized by the reigning authorities of Lower Egypt that the complete loss of Israelite laborers throughout all of Goshen would be an economic disaster, so the Egyptian army was dispatched to forcefully bring them back.

Failure of the Egyptian Army to Capture the Fleeing Israelites

It is at this point that the ancient story of Moses acquires many elements of embellishment and myth-formation. It was due to the manipulation of the anticipated reaction of the Egyptian pharaoh that Moses was able to lead an enraged army of charioteers into a marshy swamp land that sealed their destruction. Then, by other deceptive maneuvers, the fleeing Israelites were able to keep a safe distance from the pursuing Egyptian army. Moses was ultimately able to congeal the Jewish religion in line with the teachings of Abraham, Isaac, and Jacob, the belief in one true living god, and, for some, a belief in an afterlife. A massive tidal wave (tsunami) in the region of the escape path may have been blended into the story of the destruction of the Egyptian charioteers. It was physically impossible for the broad front of the Santorini-induced tidal wave to inundate one group and allow another group to escape when the two groups were separated by small distances. Also, the massive tidal wave would have followed the Santorini eruption almost immediately and would have preceded the disastrous events described in the ten plagues of Egypt. Add in many centuries of oral storytelling, and it is not surprising that many elements of historical and physical events are re-woven to produce a desired outcome.

It is also possible that the intensity of the Hebrew belief in monotheism since the time of Abraham had already set the Israelite people apart from their distant cultural and biological cousins. There were the Semitic Hyksos, who were leaning toward the pagan gods of the Egyptians, who ruled Lower Egypt at the time of the Exodus, and the Canaanites to the north who continued to believe in multiple pagan gods. The intensity of faith and beliefs of the Hebrew (Israelite) tribes was sufficient to withstand conversion by people who were likewise committed to a vast array of gods dating back thousands of years. In the process of making a complete break from the Egyptian culture and religious belief systems, Moses was intent upon refocusing the Israelite religion on a single, living god, rooting out idolatry, and, like Hammurabi before him, of crystallizing certain laws and codes of conduct for their members in a promised land of their own.

Science Versus Storytelling

Speaking as someone who personally experienced the eruption of Mt. St. Helens in the state of Washington on May 18, 1980, and then drove through the ash from Seattle to Portland, Oregon, I can tell you that the dark cloud of ash preceded everything except the explosive sounds of the eruption itself. The prevailing winds carried the ash for hundreds if not thousands of miles eastward. As the ash settled, it looked and felt exactly like dry cement mix. In places, rushing water from the rapid snow melt caused flash floods that caused the ash to build up and form hills composed only of ash and debris. Thousands of years from now that ash should still be detectable. The same is true of the massive eruption of the eastern Mediterranean island of Thera (Santorini), circa 1600 BCE. The eruption of the island now known as Santorini was 200 times more powerful than the 1980 eruption of Mt. St. Helens. The big difference between the two eruptions was that the Santorini event was far greater in magnitude and produced a very fast-moving tidal wave that would have been at least 6 to 12 feet high as it crashed upon the shores of the Nile Delta. The tidal wave and its impact on geologic factors would have preceded the ash and perhaps been associated with earthquake activity that suddenly altered the geologic factors of northern Egypt in additional catastrophic ways. Finally, considering the period of time in history and the absence of scientific information or technological means of communication, the massive, multilayered event could only be interpreted as acts of god, i.e., the one true god for the Israelites and the assorted gods of the polytheistic Egyptians.

The Massive Eruption That Changed the World

A scientific study was conducted by the Hellenic Center for Marine Research by the University of Rhode Island and the results were published in *Space & Earth Science Magazine* (August 23, 2006). During research expeditions in April and June of that year, scientists found deposits of volcanic ash that were from 11 to 86 yards thick and extended out from the island of Santorini in all directions from 6 to 50 miles. It was also noted that a much smaller volcanic eruption of Krakatoa in the Sundra Strait between the islands of Java and Sumatra in Indonesia on August 26, 1883, produced an estimated 100-foot-high tsunami. The eruption of Mt. Tambora in Indonesia in 1815, however, was about one-third larger than the Santorini eruption and had consequences felt around the world. The University of Rhode Island study also indicates that the eruption of the island of Thera (Santorini) occurred about 1600 BCE (not 1200 BCE) and likely accounts for the virtual disappearance of the highly developed Minoan culture on the nearby island of Crete as well.

First aired on April 16, 2006, on the Discovery Channel Canada, and both written and directed by Simcha Jacobovici, a new documentary on geologic forces confirms and dates the ten plagues of Egypt based on the massive eruption of the Greek island of Thera (Santorini). The focus of this well-produced, 92-minute documentary entitled "Exodus Decoded" was to confirm the revelation that the massive eruption of the eastern Mediterranean island currently known as Santorini provides a detailed geologic confirmation of events described in the book of Exodus in the Bible, and sets the date of eruption at 25 years plus or minus the year 1600 BCE. Therefore, the eruption was centuries prior to the reigns of Akhenaten and especially of Rameses II who have been erroneously associated with Moses and the Exodus out of

Egypt. Another loose association that makes little sense is to pair the Egyptian pharaoh Ahmose I with Moses because of the similarity in their Egyptian names. Ahmose I came to the throne at the age of ten years around 1550 BCE, a date that was probably many decades after the Santorini eruption. He ruled for about 25 years and his well-preserved mummy shows he died at about the age of 35 years. He is believed to have accomplished little during his brief reign, and records suggest that the Semitic Hyksos who had been ousted from the rule of Lower Egypt had been able to recapture the northern Egyptian city of Heliopolis near the end of Ahmose's first decade in power. There is a distinct absence of any surviving Egyptian records that associate Ahmose I with the biblical patriarch, Moses. Both names are Egyptian in origin, not Hebrew. The name "Moses" is a form of an Egyptian verb meaning to be born.

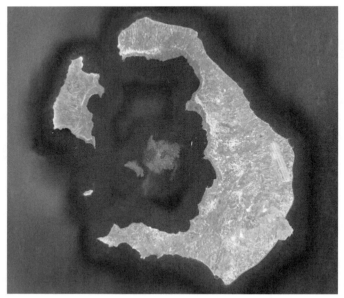

Volcanic islands of Santorini

7
Geologic Causes of the Ten Plagues of Egypt

1. Blood-Red Water

The Discovery Channel documentary entitled "Exodus Decoded" that was released in April, 2006, by Canadian director/filmmaker Simcha Jacobovici, cites the example of Lake Nyos in western Cameroon, adjacent to the African nation of Nigeria. On August 12, 1986, a seismic event turned the normally blue waters of that lake a reddish-brown color due to over-oxidation of the lake's iron-rich bottom. A cloud of deadly carbon dioxide gas was released and brought sudden death to the lake's fish and to animals and people living within 15 miles of the lake. The rapidly decaying bodies in the African heat began a sequence of disease and pestilence very comparable to the biblical description of events preceding the Exodus. Although not identical to the Santorini eruption 3,600 hundred years ago, there are many parallels to confirm the deadly similarities between those seismic events. One of the major distinctions between the two events was the existence of scientific methods and other technologies to determine causation and evacuate inhabitants to safer areas. At the end of the Bronze Age in Egypt such a catastrophic and unprecedented event could only be attributed to the wrath of gods and must have produced substantial hysteria and pure panic throughout the Delta region of northern Egypt. The iron oxide released from underground fissures was the cause for turning bodies of fresh water, including the lower end of the Nile, a reddish color and producing a toxic gas in the water sufficient to suffocate the fish and any breathing organisms nearby.

2. Infestation of Frogs
The sudden absence of millions of fish to feed on the underwater eggs of amphibians such as frogs allowed those eggs to hatch in unprecedented numbers. The result was a wholly disproportionate number of live frogs swarming throughout the Delta region in search of food. Huge numbers of frogs were being seen in areas where they had never been seen before.

3. Hordes of Gnat-like Insects, Hordes of Small Black Flies
The millions of fish that suffocated and eventually deposited themselves along the banks of the Nile and other bodies of water in the Delta region died of natural causes (toxic concentrations of carbon dioxide gas) rather than a result of chemical poisoning. The unimaginable stench was a very powerful attractant for insects and especially flies in search of fertile sources to lay their own eggs. The result of these deaths on such a large scale was the unprecedented numbers of swarming insects that quickly matured and sought food sources and spread diseases that must have been intolerable for local residents. Surely, such a pestilence could only be an expression of dissatisfaction of the gods.

4. Hordes of Horse-flies
The air was filled with large barnyard-style black flies that rampantly spread disease to humans and livestock alike.

5. Infectious Disease Spread
The combination of hot, dry weather and unprotected exposure to unimaginable hordes of flying insects feeding on the decaying bodies of fish was an inevitable source of transfer for disease to all other living organisms, especially unprotected livestock in the fields, such as cattle, sheep, goats, horses, camels, and donkeys.

6. Infectious Boils
Boils are a severe form of infected skin pores, or abscesses of the skin that are more common with exposure to unsanitary conditions. The rampant transfer of diseases of the skin from one person to another was likely a function of the extreme exposure to the vast overpopulation of flying insects after the plague of dying fish. Residences in Bronze Age Egypt typically had loose cloth coverings on doorways and windows at best and certainly lacked glass window panes, screens, and other possible defenses against impossible swarms of flying insects that were carriers of disease. Especially during difficult circumstances and given the possible spread of raw sewage by tidal waves, the sanitation practices of most ancient Egyptians after the eruption could be described as substandard at best.

7. Dirty Hail Storms
Historically, records indicated that hailstones the size of small apples pelted many regions of the Delta and were sometimes fatal to persons caught out in the open. The other distinguishing factor that was certainly related to the Minoan island of Thera (Santorini) eruption is that ash suspended in the upper atmosphere combined with unusual meteorological conditions to produce very fierce storms and bring down dirty-looking hailstones.

8. Swarms of Locusts
Infestations of locusts (a relative of the grasshopper) have been common in Africa for all of recorded history and beyond. At the time of the Exodus the locust swarms could have been part of this biological cycle, or perhaps triggered in some additional way by the seismic events that were precipitated by the eruption of the island of Thera. Either way the consequences were devastating. The voracious locust swarms consumed every bit of vegetation that the thunderous hail storms had not already de-

stroyed. Food supplies would have been limited to stored goods only, and famine was an inevitable consequence of so many combined disasters.

9. Three Days of Darkness

The size of the island of Thera (Santorini) eruption has been estimated at 200 times the magnitude of the May 18, 1980, eruption of Mt. St. Helens that dispersed ash from western Washington eastward across the United States. The result could have been sufficient ash and re-recurring ash from continuous eruptions that filled the sky with cement-like dust particles that turned day into night. Such incongruity likely terrorized any and all ancient people with the misfortune to experience such an event and created a vivid image that the gods had turned against them.

10. Death of Firstborn Egyptian Sons

Simcha Jacobovici's production, "Exodus Decoded," argues that the eruption and associated seismic activity on the island of Thera produced a ground-hugging cloud of carbon dioxide gas that was lethal only to Egyptian firstborn males. The cause was related to the Egyptian tradition of firstborn sons sleeping in a woven fiber bed that was about six inches above the ground. The bed was therefore exposed to the deadly concentration of carbon dioxide gas. All other family members and especially Israelite families slept on their rooftops at night to avoid crawling insects and especially to avoid the sudden epidemic of frogs getting into their homes. It was this final event that reportedly killed the firstborn son of the unnamed pharaoh and compelled that unidentified reigning monarch to allow approximately 5,000 to 10,000 Israelite laborers, their families, livestock, with all manner of confiscated goods and weapons to evacuate the Nile Delta.

Alternate Explanation for the Ten Plagues of Egypt

Recently, Discovery Channel's Science Channel aired a program entitled, "Plagues of Egypt." That program offered a very different interpretation of the geological/physical events summarized briefly

1. The color of blood red in the Nile and other bodies of water were attributed to red algae.
2. Massive fish kills in the Nile were related to oxygen deprivation due to the red algae.
3. The frog population exploded as they left the water and there were no fish to eat their eggs.
4. Unprecedented numbers of gnats and small flies developed due to all of the fish carcasses.
5. Horse-fly pestilence was likewise due to breeding grounds of all of the dead fish.
6. Boils and skin infections were due to excesses of flying insects being carriers of disease.
7. Dirty hail storms may have resulted because of all of the dust in the air.
8. Locust swarms may have been coincidental or triggered by sudden climatic change.
9. Three days of darkness were attributed to a dust storm after the locust damage.
10. Death of firstborn Egyptian males was attributed to a mold that formed on the top layer of grains stored in cool damp areas during a period of famine. Firstborn male children ate first. Therefore the oldest male children and largest breeding animals ate larger portions and accidentally ate the contaminated portions.

There are additional alternative explanations of geologic/physical events reported in the Bible, such as attributing the parting of the sea to a hot and dry wind storm that may have temporarily exposed a land ridge at the northern end of the Red Sea near the present site of Acuba. To evaluate that assumption more fully, it would be necessary to have an accurate topographical map and weather map of the region as it was over 3,600 years ago. No mention was made of a possible tidal wave effect that could have destroyed a major portion of the pharaoh's army, but extreme marshy conditions have typically made chariot assaults ineffective. Also, research reported on the Science Channel research suggested that Moses and his followers may have been using an erupting volcano in the vicinity of current western Saudi Arabia as a guiding reference or perhaps a ploy to confuse any Egyptian forces that were in hot pursuit. A volcanic eruption could potentially explain the pillars of fire during the night and pillars of smoke that were reported during the day.

View of modern Santorini chapel overlooking ancient volcanic caldera.

8
The Conflicting Stories of Joseph

The basic outline of the Joseph story is that he was a Hebrew or Semitic young man living in the southern area of Canaan in a family of many brothers who were competing for inheritance rights or perhaps just their father's attention. Joseph, a younger son by the wealthy father's second wife, stirred a sense of jealousy among his older brothers, when the father gave Joseph a long-sleeved coat of many bright colors, which implied that he may be the favored son. As a direct result, the half-brothers ganged up on Joseph, forcefully took his coat, and sold him as the equivalent of an indentured servant to the pharaoh's military chief, Potiphar. The brothers then smeared goat's blood on the bright-colored coat and reported to their father that Joseph had been killed.

Historically, it was not uncommon for wealthy Egyptian families to purchase household servants or laborers as indentured servants, or perhaps even as slaves, from traders with shady reputations and dubious claims to their commodities. As in the antebellum experience in the southern states of the United States, an individual with a good appearance, acceptable language skills, and a compliant nature was the preferred candidate to be a servant within the family household, and this was apparently the case with Joseph. The story, however, takes on a major dramatic twist when young Joseph acquired sufficient skills with the Egyptian language and social customs to be an object of sexual interest to Potiphar's wife. He refused her advances and in retaliation she accused him of attempted rape. Joseph was then placed in jail and while confined with two other servants, a cupbearer and a baker, he had the opportunity to interpret a dream about the meaning of three grapes crushed in a cup. Like an ancient Mesopotamian seer, Joseph made the brash claim that the dream meant a servant would be freed from jail in three days. The cupbearer was released as predicted and, at a later date, informed the pharaoh that Joseph was gifted in interpreting dreams. Considering his status as a jailed servant/slave, Joseph was almost magically given an opportunity to interpret a dream that was troubling the unidentified pharaoh.

Surviving records suggest that the significance of dreams, especially troubling dreams, in early Egypt was often taken very seriously by royal family members. Like prophecy, intuitive confirmation was especially valuable for persons of almost unlimited authority and responsibility, who supposedly had direct linkage to very powerful deities. Accurate, advance notice of a surprise attack, a killer plague, or killer famine in the form of a dream might represent survival for their people and perhaps for the royal family itself. In such a pre-science context, it is difficult to underestimate the value of a perceived psychic who can accurately interpret obscure signs, dreams, and omens. In the context of the Joseph story, however, there is also the very dramatic improbability that a foreign domestic servant, or perhaps even a slave sold into a life of bondage, would ascend from that virtually less-than-human level of existence to a position of close personal advisor of an individual who is a living link to the gods, or perhaps an actual god in his own mind.

Joseph's next opportunity came when he was asked to interpret the meaning of the pharaoh's dream about seven fat cows coming out of the Nile followed by seven thin cows. Joseph reportedly informed the (unnamed) pharaoh that the dream meant there would be seven years of prosperity followed by seven years of famine. The interpretation was taken to be valid and steps were taken to build up stores for the coming famine to lessen the devastation. The events, after a substantial interval of many years, came true as predicted; a totally devastating famine was averted and Joseph was elevated to a high-level advisory role to the pharaoh. He was given a royal signet ring and a gold chain to represent his position of authority. Confirmation of this story based on Egyptian sources appears to be lacking along with the actual name of the pharaoh. This conspicuous omission of the pharaoh's name suggests that factual elements of the story may have been tainted with storyteller's license. There is also the difficulty of placing the story in an accurate historical time frame. There is a wall carving, for instance, during the reign of Akhenaten and his queen, Nefertiti (1378-1361 BCE), that includes Chancellor Aye, a chief vizier to the pharaoh. It was the all-powerful maternal uncle, Chancellor Aye (son of Joseph), who kept Akhenaten in power, and made himself a successor to the throne as Tutankhamun's chief advisor (vizier). As an ironic result, there appears to be an historical confusion regarding Aye's father, Joseph (Yuya), and the far older story of Joseph of the Many-Colored Coat.

More Than One Old Testament Joseph?

It may be argued that two separate individuals with the common name of Joseph existed at two vastly different periods of time in Egyptian history. Joseph of the Many-Colored Coat appears to have advised the unnamed pharaoh after acquiring a high level of royal authority for a man with humble roots as a foreigner and possible slave. Perhaps it was that Joseph who encouraged a large colony of perhaps 5,000 to 10,000 of his Israelite people to return to the land of Canaan, not hundreds of thousands of fleeing refugees as is sometimes reported. The other Joseph, who appears in the Egyptian record over 200 years later, has been well-documented as a father-in-law and advisor to the pharaoh Akhenaten. This other Joseph had the Egyptian name of Yuya, and may be the man responsible for the conversion of Egypt's only monotheistic pharaoh. Over many centuries ranging from peaceful exchange to intense hostilities between the Canaanites and the Egyptians, there were intervals of much cultural exchange, and some Canaanites did achieve high office in the south on the condition that they took on the Egyptian language and manners so as not to offend the populace, the priesthood, the military, or the royal court. It is one premise of this book that it was a distinct minority of the Canaanite people who evolved into the Israelite people primarily on the basis of their solidarity and fierce belief in one living god. They adamantly stuck together as nomadic tribes throughout the regions of Canaan and Mesopotamia in spite of all opposition and being surrounded by a world of pagan gods.

Mesopotamian king or god

9
Successor to Moses and Mystery of the Promised Land
The Mystery of Ancient Jericho

One of the important factors associated with the ancient city of Jericho is the potential to re-establish a more realistic date for the Exodus. Jericho is fascinating by itself as one of the very first documented sites where early humans evolved from predominantly nomadic lives to agricultural settlements with domesticated animals, irrigation systems, sewage systems, permanent housing, and defensive walls. Jericho was ideal because of weather for growing food crops and animal feed, hillsides that could be fortified with mud bricks atop natural rock formations, and access to the Jordan River and some of its tributaries. Historical data is quite well established that this particular site to the north of the Dead Sea has been built up again and again after changes and tragedies such as earthquakes, floods, fires, famines, plagues, and invasions by outsiders. It was like a natural oasis with paradise-like conditions for the earliest Semitic people including the Canaanite people, who could also benefit from the city's location along trading routes between Egypt, the eastern Mediterranean, and the Middle East. The relative isolation away from coastal seaports and the thriving civilization of ancient Egypt was sufficient to allow the region to develop much of its own unique culture, language, and religion without constantly being at the mercy of hostile competitors in other regions.

Jericho Assimilation, Not Violent Conquest of Canaan

This oasis town in the hilly, mountainous region of the Jordan

Valley has been documented as one of the oldest human settlement sites. The availability of water made settlement a tangible possibility and something worth protecting with fortifications intended to keep roving bands of intruders from simply coming in and taking whatever they wanted. It has been estimated that during the history of Jericho mud brick walls as high as 50 feet were constructed to protect the residents of the city. The irony of the site location, however, is that the eastern edge of the city lies directly over a major fault line and was quite susceptible to earthquake damage. It was such damage that was almost certainly incorporated into the "walls came tumbling down" story perpetuated by the story of Joshua and his men invading and destroying the city and all of its residents to begin the conquest of the Canaanite people of that region. Disregarding biblical text for a moment, it is also possible that the city of Jericho was vulnerable to attack following an earthquake that severely weakened the city's defenses. It has been established in the Old Testament that Joshua, military leader and heir to Moses, intentionally selected the ancient gateway city of Jericho as the first city to attack in their strategic plan to take back the promised land from its Canaanite occupants. There is the story of Joshua and his men circling the city in force for seven days and on the seventh day using large numbers of ram's horns and other noises to "bring the walls tumbling down" prior to their invasion. Again there appears to be substantial literary license regarding the details of the invasion. First, it is improbable that a well-fortified city would be brought to its knees within a period of seven days. There is a good probability, however, that bringing the walls down could be a metaphor for using infiltration to overwhelm guards and bring down the gates to the city, which would have the same effect for the purpose of armed invasion. The coordination of large numbers of ram's horns and screaming attackers at a specific period of time could have been the signal for the infiltrators within the city to launch their attack and gain control of the gates from the inside. The story goes on to say the invasion was swift, totally effective, and that every resident was put to the sword. The message projected from such blood-lust behavior to the rest of the Canaanite people was that they would experience the same merciless fate if they did not surrender to the Israelite forces before them. Joshua's forces then continued to ravage other Canaanite cities such as Ai and Hazor to create an indelible image of the consequence for failure to yield completely to the divinely inspired Israelite forces. It may have been an embellishment to the story that a prostitute, sympathetic to the Israelite people, lived near one of the protective walls of Jericho and secretly assisted infiltrators to enter the city and open the city's gates from within upon hearing a particular signal from outside the walls.

Assimilation Rather Than Annihilation

Another potential reality for the time period of approximately 1600 BCE is that the city of Jericho had only 1,000 to 1,500 occupants at the time of the invasion. This number would have been huge during the Bronze Age period when inhabitation of cities was a new development with its own dilemmas to work out. It is also possible that Joshua took advantage of Egyptian conquests of the region in prior decades or centuries as the pendulum of hostility and hospitality would swing back and forth between the various competing cultures. The invasion may not have been a violent one but an aggressive assimilation of two competing Semitic cultures. The Canaanites and the Israelites essentially shared the roots of a common language and culture within the Near Eastern region for unknown centuries prior to this incident at Jericho. It took up to 400 years for the Israelites to conquer and to forcefully assimilate themselves into Canaan. It is also possible that the catastrophic consequences of the Santorini eruption, earthquake, and tidal waves that had facilitated the mass exodus of Semitic people out of the Delta region of Egypt impacted cities such as Jericho and completely disrupted their defenses and ability to cope with the vagaries of the environment. Thus, it could have been a collapse of the old order due to mass immigration of new peoples with a tenacious belief in a living god over residents of similar genetic backgrounds who persisted with pagan traditions and beliefs. The accounts of mass extermination down to the last child may have been an early use of negative, terrorist propaganda intended to instill overwhelming fear. Canaanite communities still resisted the Israelite onslaught during the roughly 400-year period required to completely subjugate and assimilate with the existing Canaanite residents. A blatant hypocrisy among the first or second generation of the followers of Moses who had introduced ten specific commandments that had parallels with laws described in the Egyptian Book of the Dead is the literal disregard for the commandment to not kill.

Conflicting Dates for the Origin of Monotheism

There are few reliable sources for dating events in antiquity. Some events are not reported in accurate chronological order. Some events are more myth and political fabrication than real. Surviving records left by political or religious scribes dating back thousands of years were not objective, unbiased statements based on reliable sources. In almost all instances, it is not known who the writer was, and failure to record events as instructed by authoritarian figures with the power of life and death over the scribe would have predictably bad consequences, such as immediate execution. This is true of the biblical story of Joseph of the

Coat of Many-Colors. It has been calculated by some researchers that the story may have been transmitted orally for many centuries and was not committed to a surviving written format for hundreds of years after the fact. Allen Lloyd, Egyptologist, has suggested that the story of Joseph the Patriarch preceded Moses by at least four centuries. Another respectable Egyptologist, Ahmen Osman, in his book, *Moses and Akhenaten*, made the claim that Joseph (Yuya) had a contemporaneous influence upon the pharaoh Akhenaten and that the Exodus occurred along with the disappearance or demise of Akhenaten about 1361 BCE. Mr. Osman makes the claim that Akhenaten escaped death and the humiliation of exile by transforming himself into Moses.

Ancient Egypt's Brief Brush with Monotheism

The Egyptian pharaoh, Amenhotep III, ascended to the throne of both Upper and Lower Egypt in the year 1386 BCE. The distinctive Egyptian civilization had been in place for approximately 2,000 years and had been ruled by at least 84 different pharaohs (kings) by that time. It was a period of relative tranquility and great affluence that allowed the new pharaoh to embark upon massive building projects including embellishment of the ancient temple in Thebes dedicated to Amun, the Egyptian lord of creation, and the beginnings of the magnificent Hypostyle Hall with its massive and distinctive columns. The Colossi of Memnon statuary that represents Amenhotep III also includes a standing image of his wife, Queen Tiye, poised on a diminished scale but suggesting great importance to him and the people of Egypt. It is believed that she exerted a very positive influence on her husband and pharaoh at a time when women were typically lacking in influence in any realm of the empire except child rearing and homemaking. One major distinction was that Tiye's parents, Yuya (i.e., Joseph), a commander of chariotry under Thutmose IV, and his wife, Thuya, were believed to be of Semitic origin, among Egypt's elite classes, and may have converted their daughter to monotheism. Such a conversion would have been unprecedented, spiked with dangers, and a radically different religious philosophy within a two-thousand-year-old Egyptian civilization. Queen Tiye had been associated with the cult of the deified Ahmose Nefertari, and she may have privately shared her radical beliefs with her husband, and especially with her second son, Amenhotep IV (Akhenaten), as he was frail, disfigured, and one who acquired obsessive interests in theological philosophy with little anticipation of ascending to the position of pharaoh. His older brother, Thutmose V, was the crown prince, and the one being groomed to be the next pharaoh until his unexpected death.

Amenhotep III is typically credited with initiating construction of the Temple of Amun, major reconstruction within the Temple of Luxor and the Karnak Temple Complex, including the Hypostyle Temple with 134 gargantuan columns and a ceiling height of 74 feet. He is also considered to be responsible for construction of the Avenue of Rams Head Sphinxes at Karnak. Amenhotep III was interred in the western section of the Valley of Kings in close proximity to the tomb of his vizier and high priest, Aye. It was Aye, the pharaoh's Semitic brother-in-law, who served in the same position during the reign of Akhenaten, and then as the co-regent of Tutankhamun. This elderly top advisor to three different pharaohs succeeded in ascending to the throne following the sudden and possibly unexpected death of the 19-year-old boy-king in 1323 BCE.

The tomb of Amenhotep III was first discovered in 1799 by Napoleon's soldiers (KV 22). It was severely damaged by water and salt leaching into the stone and most wall decorations had fallen or were beyond recognition. His tomb had been looted and almost everything of possible historical value had been stripped away. Amenhotep's reign occurred at a peaceful time when there was little military activity and more opportunity to focus on the arts and philosophical issues such as religion. He consolidated the power of his throne by marrying the daughters of foreign kings, and may have had as many as 317 total wives and concubines. His chief and favorite wife, Queen Tiye, assumed a more important role in the pharaoh's life than had been the case before her reign. They were married as adolescents since Amenhotep III came to the throne at the approximate age of 13 years and reigned for a period of 37 years. Before dying of possible infections brought on by serious dental problems at the age of 50 years, he was in a position to be quite sexually active and may have acted as a surrogate for his probably sterile son, Amenhotep IV (Akhenaten). There is some reason to believe that he was also the possible father of Smenkhkare, who later succeeded Akhenaten for as little as a few days, and has been represented as being quite effeminate. It has been argued that Queen Nefertiti disguised herself as a male pharaoh by the name of Smenkhkare to preserve her life and her royal position. Possibly, the DNA studies reported in the February 17, 2010, issue of the Journal of the American Medical Association will help to clarify the actual lineage of this long-standing royal mystery.

Amenhotep III encouraged monument construction at a time of flourishing trade with sources outside of Egypt. One of his most spectacular public works was the huge memorial temple at Kawm el-Hitan on the controversial western bank of the Nile. It was there that two imposing 66-foot statues of Amenhotep III, known as the Colossi of Memnon, were erected as the entrance or pylon (gates) to his mortuary temple. These statues have been severely damaged over time and are subject to collapse if an earthquake should occur. These very impressive statues represent the only recognizable feature to the entry of Akhenaten's radical new temple city of Tell el-Amarna which was later systematically demolished and carted off, block by block under the orders of the Oppressor Pharaoh, Horemheb, in a public effort to stamp out all trace of Akhenaten's new religion of the sun god, Aten, and all memory of the four pharaohs prior to Horemheb, i.e., Amenhotep IV (Akhenaten), Smenkhkare, Tutankhamun, and Aye.

Nefertiti (left) and Akhenaten

10
Egypt's Centrist Position for Early Religion

The importance of Egypt's centralized location for the beginnings of human civilization was immeasurable. Essential cities developed along the major north-south trade routes represented by the Nile. In the northeastern Delta region just south of Canaan (presently Israel and Palestine) was the coastal fortress city of Avaris (Tell el-Daba) near Pa-Rameses, an essential city for the major Israelite settlement of ancient times known in the Bible as Goshen. For many centuries Semitic people had migrated to and from the area with relatively little resistance as long as their numbers did not represent a political or military threat to the Egyptian hierarchy. A little further to the south was the ancient capital of Memphis, which was especially active during the Old Kingdom (2650-2134 BCE) and near the Giza Plateau and the Sphinx. Stunning temple cities included Abydos, Memphis, Thebes (including the massive temples of Karnak and now known as Luxor), and Akhetaten (Tell el-Amarna), site of Akhenaten's new capital of Egypt and the monotheistic religion he founded. The very ancient city of Abydos was once a capital of Upper and Lower Egypt and the mythological home of Osiris, the god of the underworld, all vegetation, and of resurrection after death. Other significant areas further up the Nile were Elephantine Island, Aswan, the First Cataract, and then the southern border with the kingdom of Kush (ancient home of the Nubian people), and the most impressive monuments of Abu Simbel which were built during the reign of Rameses II. These magnificent works of religious/political art were carved out of the side of a limestone mountain and constructed on a grandiose scale. The seated statues would be over one hundred feet tall if in a standing position. The purpose was for Rameses II to glorify and deify himself, his wife, Queen Nefertari (not the same as Akhenaten's wife, Queen Nefertiti), and to intentionally awe and intimidate the mineral-rich Nubian people of Kush. That region to the south of Egypt is currently known as Somalia and Ethiopia.

In the long historical view, Egypt can be considered the crossroads of the earliest nomads of the human race from Africa to the rest of the world. The agrarian paradise of the Nile Valley was bordered by hazardous, almost lifeless deserts and mountains to the east and west and natural borders of the Red Sea and Mediterranean Sea. It was the ideal setting for Egyptian culture to grow, evolve, and make major and often unprecedented impacts on the remainder of the world. The broader concept of "cradle of civilization" is equally applicable to Egypt as to early Sumerian/Akkadian culture in the Tigris and Euphrates valleys. The early civilizations were in close enough proximity to influence each other on a regular basis. It is considered by many to be a futile exercise to say that one civilization preceded the other.

Ancient Egyptian Stele

11
The Semitic Contribution to Egyptian Monotheism

The evolution of Egypt included the development of folklore, mythology, and religion that produced hundreds of gods and goddesses during a period of about 3,000 years up to the time of the death of Cleopatra and Mark Anthony, and the rise of Christianity. Incidentally, the probable burial site of the last Ptolemy queen and her Roman lover appears to have been discovered in a deep shaft under the ruins of an old temple in Alexandria in the month of April, 2009. During those three millennia there was one interval of seventeen years when all Egyptian gods and goddesses were discredited and replaced by a single, omniscient god, the sun god, Aten. It was during the controversial reign of Akhenaten (c. 1378-1361 BCE) that the entire pantheon of deities was cast to the winds by a very unlikely pharaoh and his beautiful wife and queen, Nefertiti. Historical evidence is sketchy but suggests that Akhenaten was influenced and perhaps wholly converted to the concept of a single god by his maternal grandfather-in-law, Joseph, Egyptian name Yuya, and his grandmother-in-law, Thuya. This is not the same Joseph who was reportedly sold into Egyptian slavery by his brothers and later became a senior minister to an unnamed pharaoh by translating the monarch's dream to mean there would be seven good years followed by seven bad years. It is a premise of this book that Joseph (Yuya) persuaded the very eccentric and perhaps genetically disabled future king of Egypt to accept the Israelite concept of a single god in place of literally hundreds of Egyptian gods and goddesses that had been worshipped in one way or another for two thousand years. Among the immediate consequences of Akhenaten's conversion was the complete disruption of perhaps 5,000 priests who were given the option to accept the sun god, Aten, or be completely displaced. The military, headed by Horemheb, and Akhenaten's maternal uncle, Chancellor Aye, had the responsibility of controlling sufficient elements of the palace guard and the priesthood to protect the royal family from the disenfranchised and rebellious priests and others throughout Egypt who continued to believe in the ancient pantheon of gods and goddesses. The aging Chancellor Aye was able to accomplish this extraordinary feat by maintaining a loyal, armed camp within Akhenaten's newly built temple city of Akhetaten (Tell el-Amarna).

Joseph (Yuya) and Thuya (parents of Aye and Queen Tiye)

The Semitic Maternal In-laws of Akhenaten and Nefertiti

The name Joseph, being a common Hebrew name and not typical of the Egyptian language, may be a major source of confusion in the story of Moses and the story of Akhenaten. Ironically, there is a distinct argument to be made that Akhenaten transformed himself into the new identity of Moses at the time of being dethroned. The simplistic logic is that being the leader of the only monotheist religion in Egypt, Akhenaten aligned with the Israelites of Goshen and led them to the promised land during the year of 1336 BCE (plus or minus about two years). That time period, however, does not begin to align with the massive eruption of the island of Thera (Santorini) that produced physical and geological events that match exactly with the biblical description of the ten plagues of Egypt more than two hundred years earlier. It is the opinion of this writer that an earlier Joseph (Joseph of the Many-Colored Coat) was a contemporary or near contemporary of Moses, and that he facilitated Moses in leading the exodus of perhaps 10,000 Hebrew men, women, children, and livestock out of Egypt shortly after the massive eruption of the island of Thera. It was a separate event when Joseph, or Yuya, and his wife, Thuya, contributed to the possible conversion of Amenhotep III and facilitated the major conversion of his son, Akhenaten, to become ancient Egypt's only monotheist king (c. 1378-1361 BCE). Perhaps the historical record will someday give full credit to the Hebrew people for adherence to a single living god many centuries prior to a maximum seventeen-year failed experiment with monotheism that can be attributed to Akhenaten and his maternal grandfather-in-law and maternal grandmother-in-law.

Yuya was the Egyptian equivalent for the Hebrew name, Joseph, which may have been easier to pronounce in the Egyptian language. By one account, Yuya has been described as a wealthy landowner and priest from the Upper Egyptian town of Akhmin. By another account, he was the commander of chariotry under Thutmose IV. He has also been described as being non-Egyptian in appearance, i.e., Syrian or "Asiatic," meaning he was likely of Semitic or Near Eastern descent. His existence has been further confirmed based on skeletal factors of his mummy. Yuya's existence and importance to both Amenhotep III and to the latter's son, Akhenaten, was demonstrated by his being mummified and entombed in the Valley of the Kings when they were otherwise just the non-Egyptian parents of Queen Tiye (wife of Amenhotep III). Joseph's wife, Thuya (also spelled Tuya, Tjuya, or Thuyu) was also accorded high status and was associated with various religious cults based on various titles given to her and found in her well-preserved tomb within the Valley of the Kings.

12
Akhenaten, the Heretic King

Akhenaten can be described as the most eccentric, most improbable, and most controversial pharaoh in 3,000 years of ancient Egyptian history. His total reign was for a maximum period of approximately seventeen years. The initial portion of Akhenaten's reign may have been shared with his father, Amenhotep III, as a co-regent and the last few months or days of his reign may have been shared with his cousin or half-brother, Semenkhkare. It remains unverified, but there were strong indications that Akhenaten was assassinated in the process of being unceremoniously dethroned. The heretic pharaoh and his famous wife, queen, and half-sister, Nefertiti, totally upset complicated belief systems that had been in place for two thousand years of Egyptian history. They were the heretic monarchs who discredited all of the existing gods and goddesses of Egypt in favor of a monotheistic belief in the sun god, Aten. The process of introducing a radically new belief system was abrupt and totally confrontational to the priests and inhabitants of Egypt, who were not in any way prepared to make such a change. One of the surprises was that Akhenaten was able to implement this radical new belief system for a period of seventeen years before being mysteriously ousted. Because he was a weak child, it was only through the strength and political power of his mother, Queen Tiye, and father, King Amenhotep III, that he assumed power as the heretic pharaoh. The true sustaining force of Akhenaten's unpopular reign can be credited to his maternal uncle, Chancellor Aye, who held the old priesthood at bay and controlled the palace guard as a virtual armed camp.

Genetic Disorders Associated with Royal Inbreeding

Akhenaten may have been a victim of Froehlich's syndrome. This disorder is exacerbated by royal inbreeding and is due to a hypothalamic disorder or a tumor of the anterior pituitary gland. Symptoms tend to include underdeveloped genitals, development of feminine secondary sexual characteristics, and lowered body temperature, or lowered blood pressure. Impotence and/or sterility would have been very probable and devastating for anyone in the position of being a hereditary male king. In the historic record there are indications that Akhenaten was considered the father of six daughters and one son, Tutankhaten (Tutankhamun). However, there is reason to believe the actual father of the seven children was Akhenaten's father, Amenhotep III, not a royal surrogate according to recent DNA studies. The pressure to preserve royal lineage and the illusion that the genetically disabled pharaoh had the virility to perform all of his functions as a hereditary monarch was critical.

Akhenaten was apparently not a victim of a genetic disorder called Marfan's syndrome which can be associated with inbreeding within royal families where marriage of a sister or first cousin was perceived to strengthen the royal blood line, along with increased claims to the throne, rather than weaken it. The historic evidence for an overly feminine appearance in a male pharaoh was the radical departure of Egyptian art during his reign, which was known as the Amarna Period. Artistic images were much more relaxed and less stylized than Egyptian art forms before or after his reign. Sculpted images of Akhenaten show elongated and narrow features of his face, fingers, broadened hips, and probable breast development typical of that syndrome. He is understood to have been a sickly child who was not expected to live a full life and was not trained in the arts of war and other evidence of physical prowess that was typical of a pharaoh. He appears to have been quite sheltered by a powerful queen-mother Tiye, wife of Amenhotep III. Both parents would have been under great pressure to ensure a future male descendant for the throne to avoid possible civil war. Amenhotep's long reign may have included several years as a co-regent with his son, Akhenaten. The genetically disabled pharaoh reigned on his own for perhaps twelve of the seventeen years usually attributed to him. Finally, as pressure over the disruptive monotheism erupted, Akhenaten is believed to have ruled with his half-brother, or perhaps a cousin, Semenkhkare, for a period of only months or days. The real power behind the throne (Chancellor/vizier Aye and General of the Armies Horemheb) were intent on preventing a failure of the monarchy and a coup d'etat from the military, the displaced priesthood, or the dissenting population of Egypt. The urgency to change back to the traditional belief systems of the very powerful priesthood was such that the two brothers were not going to be allowed to serve out their reign as co-regents. Instead, Akhenaten's son, Tutankhamun (originally Tutankhaten), or perhaps his half-brother if fathered by Amenhotep III and one of Akhenaten's secondary wives, Queen Kiya, ascended to the throne. As the only legal heir to the throne, Tut was pressed into accepting the position of pharaoh at the age of 9 or 10 years. Tutankhamun's father, or perhaps half-brother, Akhenaten, was in all probability assassinated or at least forced into permanent and secret exile. Akhenaten's half-brother and co-regent, Semarkhkare, was pressured to relocate to the old capital of Thebes and was believed to have been unceremoniously dispatched within the first few days or months after his forced transfer to Thebes. Akhenaten's newly built capital of Amarna was totally discredited and entered into the process of being systematically dismantled. The surviving Queen Nefertiti, who may have clandestinely used surrogates to father her six daughters to cover-up Akhenaten's possible sterility, was not allowed to remain in power due to her total association with the religion of the Aten. She was held in contempt by most of the real powers behind the throne and was not allowed to serve as Tutankhamun's regent. The ultimate fate of this beautiful queen is almost as mysterious as the disappearance of her radical-pharaoh husband. It is known that King Tut's young wife, Ankhesenamun, suspected the elderly vizier, Aye, in the death of her husband and was repulsed by the likelihood that she was obligated to marry him to retain her position as the queen of Egypt. There is evidence that she failed in an attempt to marry one of the adult sons of Hittite King Shuppilulima prior to the end of the ritualized burial period of her deceased husband. The Hittite royal prince was murdered as he was about to cross the Egyptian border, by Egyptian loyalists wanting to restore the traditional Amun religion. The result of the extreme religious upheaval was a brief co-regency with elderly vizier Aye being the absolute and virtually exclusive advisor to Tutankhamun. Ultimately, there was a controversial, sudden, and probably accidental death of the boy-king at the age of 19 years. Forensic evidence that Tutankhamun was murdered during a late puberty cover-up of a genetic disorder has become very improbable. The now documented cause of death was rampant infection in an adolescent's body with a weakened immune system due to also having the most lethal form of malaria tropica in his system.

New documentation of Tutankhamun's death as recently as February, 2010, has been based upon a scientific evaluation of the boy-king's mummy that was observed by Egypt's Chief Archeologist, Dr. Zahi Hawass, who heads the Supreme Council of

Antiquities in Cairo. The evaluation was conducted at the Museum of Egyptian Antiquities in Cairo. The medical opinion is that the 19-year-old male appeared to have a weakened immune system due to a virulent form of malaria tropica that attacks the cerebral area and is the most deadly form of the disease. Additional documentation showed a severe break of his left leg, partial healing, and a high probability of death due to infection. In addition, the mummy showed some characteristics that may have been associated with many generations of royal inbreeding. There was evidence of a bone disorder known as Kohler disease II, some deformity of his left foot, and he was also afflicted with avascular bone necrosis of the ball of his foot that would have been quite painful and necessitated the use of a cane or walking stick. A total of 113 well-used walking sticks were found in Tut's tomb. Among the other curiosities was the absence of any evidence that the heart had been left in the body to fulfill one of the rites of passage into a pharaoh's afterlife. He had been rather sloppily coated in resin at two different times. His arms were not arranged in the traditional pose of a pharaoh and there is little evidence that he was a robust military leader as a pharaoh, or an aggressive chariot driver as some have suggested. Evidence of feminine characteristics that may have been inherited from the royal family was either not confirmed or not confirmable. The presence of coriander seeds in his tomb suggests a possible use for treatment of fever prior to his death, and the broken chariot parts found within the tomb suggest an accidental fall as he would have been quite unstable on his feet. Projecting a virulent image of a godlike warrior pharaoh would have been progressively more difficult, and if clear signs of feminine characteristics were evident, it might have been impossible to cover up.

Conversion to the In-law's Monotheistic Religion

The claim has been made that Akhenaten was the first monotheistic Egyptian king, and a case can be made that he was converted as a young man by his maternal grandfather, Joseph (Yuya). To make sense of that claim, however, it is necessary to document the existence of two very different Semitic men of great influence within the Egyptian royal family by the name of Joseph. Otherwise, it is necessary to substantially distort the known historical calendar by many centuries to make it appear that the Exodus of Moses occurred as a result of Akhenaten's failed reign and that Akhenaten transformed himself into Moses and led the Israelites out of the northeastern Delta of Egypt. It is claimed by the respected author, Ahmed Osman, in *Moses and Akhenaten*, that the Exodus preceded the reign of the Oppressor Pharaoh Horemheb. He was the old military leader who forcefully made himself the last king of the Eighteenth Dynasty following the possibly controversial death of Aye. As the pharaoh's chief adviser (vizier) and high priest, Aye directly influenced the military protection and control necessary to protect the heretic king, Akhenaten. The newly created capital and temple to the sun god, Aten, was a virtual armed camp and there is little evidence that the populace or the power of the military, bureaucracy, or the priesthood ever accepted the Aten as their sole god. The four Amarna kings were Akhenaten, Smenkhkare, Tutankhamun, and Aye. Much of the official record of the four Amarna kings was systematically destroyed by Aye's successor, General of the Armies Horemheb, when he ascended the throne upon Aye's death. There was a systematic effort on the part of a vast majority of Egyptians, especially the displaced priesthood, to destroy the heretical religion of the new sun god, Aten, and to eliminate the radically different monarchy that had replaced two thousand years of faith in gods and goddesses with a single all-powerful god.

Royal Genetic Frailties

Much attention has been given to the possibility that Akhenaten may have been impotent due to a genetic disorder known as Froehlich's Syndrome or Marfan's Syndrome. The DNA study reported in the February 17, 2010, issue of JAMA, however, did rule out Marfan's. However, the historical record that Akhenaten had six daughters by Queen Nefertiti and a son, Tutankhaten, by a lesser wife, Queen Kiya, who may have been fathered by Amenhotep III, but definitely not a surrogate within the royal court. The pressure on a living monarch to produce a suitable male heir was enormous, and, in some respects his situation was similar to that of Henry VIII, who challenged the authority of the Roman Catholic Church. Akhenaten challenged the authority of the Egyptian priesthood and a complex, 2,000-year-old Egyptian belief system. The pressures were great to protect a good many secrets within royal families that could produce children by multiple wives, blood relatives, in-laws, concubines, and with little chance that the Egyptian public could make a claim to the contrary. The JAMA study indicated above describes an updated autopsy of Tutankhamun's mummy that was completed with the famed Egyptologist, Dr. Zahi Hawass, present. It was concluded that the most probable cause of death was due to widespread infection following a broken leg as the immediate cause and traces of malaria tropica in his system as a contributing factor to the young man's death. It was further noted that the 19-year-old king was born with a cleft palate, a club foot that likely required a cane or crutch for walking, but no mention of possible Frolich's syndrome. The adverse consequence of royal in-breeding does not seem to set well with the image of a glorious Egyptian civilization lasting over 3,000 years. There can be no doubt that Akhenaten was grossly impacted by genetic defects and perhaps a sweltering resentment of the traditional gods that allowed this to happen to such a royal personage. Tutankhamun may likewise have harbored resentments about such visible imperfections as a young boy with a royal, if not divine, image to uphold. The final straw for the powers behind the throne that may have been very difficult to understand were the possible secondary sexual characteristics of a female as the young king progressed through adolescence. Another possibility is that some of the statuary found in Tutankhamun's tomb that shows clear feminine characteristics were items intended for the tomb of his step-mother, Nefertiti, not the physical image of a male pharaoh with a feminine body.

Akhenaten's Doomed City of Amarna

Virtually lost and forgotten until the Eighteenth Century CE, the once-beautiful temple complex and royal seat of the god, Aten, rivaled the nearby temples of Thebes (Luxor). The heretic pharaoh Akhenaten and his queen, Nefertiti, symbolically and figuratively upset a 2,000- to 3,000-year-old Egyptian culture that was obsessed with maintaining order and displaying great reverence for a complex array of gods and goddesses. The heretic pharaoh undertook a completely radical departure by ordering the construction of an entirely new temple-city dedicated to a single unpopular god. Akhenaten went even further when he declared himself the living link to that omniscient god of Egypt and, short of declaring himself a deity, Akhenaten appointed Meryre II as the high priest of Aten. The break from absolutely rigid tradition was so great that the temple complex and city of Amarna was laid out and built not only on barren ground in a natural amphitheater setting, but on the far less inhabited western side of the Nile. It was the side where the sun set each evening and gave off the mystic illusion of dying each evening only to be reborn each morning in the east. Even 5,000 years later, most development and habitation is on the eastern side of the Nile and the deceased are typically buried on the western side.

Creation of a New Temple City on the Opposite Bank of the Nile

Akhenaten's temple city and new Egyptian capital of Amarna was built to rival or exceed the ancient capital of Thebes (Luxor) in every respect and to be the new capital of his reign. In major ways the huge complex was built to be awe-inspiring and not to be another rote tribute to the old gods of Egypt. The exquisite temple city had an entirely new focus on a single omniscient god. It is the opinion of this writer that the sun god, Aten, was modeled on the pre-existing Israelite concept of a living god, and not conceived by Akhenaten alone. Also, it was likely that Amenhotep III and his wife, Queen Tiye, may have been privately converted to Egyptian monotheism by Yuya (Joseph) and Thuya (parents of Queen Tiye) without taking the risk of going public as did their son, Akhenaten. Thus, with image and grandiosity being major hallmarks of Egyptian authority, many elements for the planned city of Amarna were designed on a truly grand scale. The speed with which everything was constructed, however, resulted in many of the workers' homes and supportive businesses being constructed in a haphazard manner simply as space was available. Occupancy by the pharaoh and his family occurred during the fifth year of his reign. The magnificent temple city, complete with palaces, temples, government buildings, storehouses, businesses, and the Altar of Aten, was also a virtual military encampment to protect the exceedingly controversial and unpopular royal family. It was the pharaoh's maternal great-uncle, Aye, who commanded the military palace guard and was the protector of the heretical family that would reign for a total of 17 years before being unceremoniously uprooted and likely assassinated or forced into permanent exile and obscurity. It was Aye, the elderly vizier and high priest who became the regent for Tutankhamun, a boy of about 9 to 10 years of age. King Tut was next in line to be pharaoh. He was compelled to change his name from Tutankhaten to Tutankhamun and to restore the ancient master god of Amun-Ra. All of the ancient gods and goddesses were ceremoniously reinstated to avoid total civil war and the possible collapse of the monarchy. Before the pre-pubescent king was placed upon the throne, however, his father (or perhaps his half-brother), Akhenaten and Semenkhkare, are believed to have both met a violent end in the intense religious backlash that displaced ancient Egypt's only monotheistic monarchy. The old religious structure of Egypt was immediately restored under the combination of aging Chancellor/vizier Aye and the boy-king, renamed, Tutankhamun. The temple city of Amarna was systematically dismantled and leveled to the point of being unrecognizable and forgotten to most of history. The four kings of the Amarna Period- Akhenaten, Semenkhkare, Tutankhamun, and Aye- were officially de-listed from the Egyptian Books of Kings at Abydos by the self-appointed tough old general, Horemheb, who declared himself a king (the word "pharaoh," which generally referred to "the house of," was generally not used during ancient times). It was Horemheb, known as the Oppressor Pharaoh, who appointed Rameses I, another old warrior/politician, to be his successor. He was the next pharaoh for less than two years and was succeeded by his son, Seti (Seti I), who was among the first to declare himself a deity and eventually passed on the throne to his son, Rameses II, who likewise declared himself a deity. Even Rameses II, many generations after Akhenaten, joined in the melee by ordering the removal of cut stones from Amarna to be moved across the Nile for the construction of his own buildings. Final desecration of the virtually unrecognizable city founded about 1,350 BCE was continued by the Coptic Christians about two to three centuries after the death of Jesus Christ. Entry to the almost totally demolished city is still guarded by two colossal yet defaced statues that are 66 feet tall and known as the Colossi of Memnon.

The Speculation That Akhenaten Became Moses

Sigmund Freud (1856-1939) wrote a book called *Moses and Monotheism* that was published in March, 1939. The "groundbreaking" book quickly became obscure following Hitler's invasion of Poland in September, 1939, due to the systematic persecution and execution of Jews and others targeted by the Nazi Party. Freud, a world-famous psychoanalyst, was struck by the first and only introduction of monotheism to ancient Egypt by a single pharaoh. He speculated that Moses was not a Jew but an Egyptian of high standing who was associated with the brief reign of Akhenaten. Parallels of religious rebellion have been frequent in the world's history where social upheavals tend to be lead by affluent intellectuals rather than rising stars among the downtrodden. The Moses described by Freud was likely a ranking Egyptian priest who had frequent access to the ideologies and sufferings of the Hebrew people working under miserable conditions in the northeastern Delta region of Lower Egypt. The acid test, however, is that a physically and mentally strong leader with access to the unnamed pharaoh would be required to inspire a major community of perhaps 5,000 to 10,000 "illegal alien" workers and persuade them to abandon their jobs, their homes, and risk their lives by leaving Egypt all at once.

Akhenaten or Moses Living to the Age of 120 Not Likely

A genetically and physically weak Akhenaten would not have had the physical strength to assume the leadership role of Moses to plan and implement the exodus of an entire Hebrew community in a hostile environment and outmaneuver an unnamed pharaoh's pursuing army. The actual Moses had to be a physically tough and brilliant military commander as well as a charismatic leader. It is not realistic that the Moses of the Old Testament, who has been described as living to the age of 120 years, launched such an arduous military campaign at the age of 80 years and proceeded to survive in the desert wilderness for another 40 years. Mythologizing one of history's most significant events simply diminishes one of the biggest watershed events in all of human history. The assumption that Moses and Akhenaten were one and the same person is tempting to consider but can have no validity in the real world. The details of the disappearance of Akhenaten at the abrupt end of his seventeen-year reign have not been found in the Egyptian record. Unlike royal personages up to the time of Akhenaten, evidence is lacking that he received the funerary rites accorded to a pharaoh. The new religion of the Aten cast aside the earlier concepts of sacred preparations for the afterlife. The rock-cut tombs associated with the elite of Akhenaten's administration were distinctly different from those at Thebes or other historic sites in Egypt. Whatever final respect that may have been shown for "the heretic" pharaoh was intentionally defiled and erased to the extent possible under the orders of Pharaoh Horemheb, Akhenaten's Commander of the Armies, and successor to the brief reigns of Tutankhamun and his co-regent, Aye. Horemheb, the Oppressor Pharaoh, reigned from approximately 1323-1292 BCE, and did all within his power to stamp out what has become known as the Amarna period.

The tomb of Queen Nefertiti and several royal family members (Yuya and Thuya), however, was recently found and identified beyond a reasonable doubt, but not accepted by Dr. Zahi Hawass. Desecration of Nefertiti's mummy (a smashed mouth and damaged chest cavity) suggests extreme animosity toward her by apparent tomb robbers and the attempt to disrupt her afterlife, especially by the temporarily disenfranchised priesthood.

The connection between Akhenaten and the specific identity of the man known to the world as Moses would have been far too big of a story for early writers of the Old Testament to ignore. The Moses of the Exodus, being of Hebrew origin, first had to achieve a high level of acceptance and trust within Egypt's royal family. He had to be a most extraordinary man capable of assuming great leadership positions in both the Egyptian and Hebrew worlds. In the New Testament (Acts 7 22) the statement is made, "And Moses was learned in all of the wisdom of the Egyptians, and he was mighty in words and deeds." This comment implies that a foreigner, not a native-born royal court member, had excelled in acquiring and understanding the Egyptian culture and intricacies of the royal hierarchy. Further Bible references indicate that Moses was outside Egypt when he and his brother, Aaron the Levite, were instructed by the God of Abraham to return to Egypt and lead the Hebrews to the Promised Land. Freud also alluded to the writings of a priest and advisor to the Greek-era Pharaoh, Ptolemy I, by the name of Manetho. In his *History of Egypt* written approximately 300 years prior to the birth of Christ, Manetho described Moses as a high-ranking Egyptian priest who had been educated in the Lower Egypt city of Heliopolis. Thus, based on such loose threads of information, Freud sought to make a connection between the heretic, sickly pharaoh Akhenaten and the Egyptian priest of foreign extraction named Moses as being one and the same person. What Sigmund Freud lacked, however, was documentation of the massive eruption of the island of Thera that accounts for all of the Ten Plagues of Egypt and sets the historical clock back approximately 300 years. Also, with Tut's death occurring more than two centuries after the probable time of the actual Exodus, it is totally improbable that Tut was the "unnamed" pharaoh of the Old Testament's Exodus. Nor was Tut, a teenage boy, in a position to lead an assault against possibly 5,000 to 10,000 fleeing Israelites, and he obviously didn't die in the returning flood waters of a possibly Santorini-induced tidal wave over the marshes of the Reed Sea, or perhaps the northern end of the Red Sea.

Tutankhamun death mask and funerary images

13
Power Surge to Restore Egyptian Paganism

The mysteries surrounding the disappearance and/or death of Akhenaten may never be resolved with a high level of acceptance by researchers and interested public alike. The Egyptian government, in fact, appears to have grown weary of the horror associated with the heretic king who reigned for a maximum of seventeen years in the midst of at least 3,000 years of continuous and often wondrous cultural history up to the time of Jesus Christ and for another 2,000 years up to the present. Until recently, the Egyptian government has been reluctant to do a DNA study of a possible mummy of Akhenaten, or the certain carbonized mummy of Tutankhamen. However, a great deal of information is available about the boy-king who succeeded Akhenaten at the age of approximately nine or ten years. Recent DNA testing has established the kinship with the apparent mummy of Akhenaten and therefore squashed the powerful rumor that he assumed the identity of Moses upon being forced to abdicate his throne at a very precise date in recorded history. DNA testing has validated the actual kinship of the boy-king, Tutankhamun.

This is important in a variety of ways. First, there has been much uncertainty in the royal succession lineage whether Tut was the biological son of Akhenaten, as indicated at the time, or perhaps a surrogate parent. The uncertainty and reason for doubt was due to Akhenaten's genetic disorder(s), which likely rendered him sterile in a situation where producing at least one viable male heir was paramount to his position of king of Upper and Lower Egypt. Second, there is the complication that Akhenaten had a very sheltered upbringing due to his apparent disorders by his powerful mother, Queen Tiye. Third, there is the potential for additional genetic liability within the royal family when Akhenaten was married to his half-sister, the beautiful Nefertiti. Fourth, it appears on the surface to be something of an over exaggeration to stress that the marriage of Akhenaten and Nefertiti had produced six healthy daughters as well. Fifth, the DNA testing appears to confirm that the real father of Tutankhamun was Akhenaten, not the boy-king's grandfather, Amenhotep III. The mother of Tutankhamun was Akhenaten's secondary wife, Queen Kiya, not the more famous Queen Nefertiti and the potential for incest never goes away. The mummies found in KV55 and KV35YL have been identified as the parents of Tutankhamun. Genetic testing of the Y chromosome alleles revealed identical patterns in Amenhotep III, Akhenaten, and Tutankhamun. Finally, DNA testing did confirm the existence of one or more genetic disorders that would be progressively evident as Tut aged further and further past initial puberty. The Freiberg-Kohler syndrome was considered to be active at the time of Tutankhaumn's death. Other disorders, such as gynecomastia and Marfan syndrome, were ruled out on the basis of well formed genitalia and absence of the elongated skull typical of Marfan's. A male king who is the physical and divine representative of all Egyptians could not survive if he progressively took on more and more secondary sexual characteristics of a woman. The gods, even in a state of transition, would not have made such an error. Sculptures found in Tutankhamun's tomb, which are clearly effeminate, may have been images of Queen Nefertiti or simply artistic license of the Amarna period.

Controversy over Tutankhamun's Premature Death

It is the understanding of this writer that the current Egyptian government is satisfied to end the debate that Tutankhamun may or may not have been murdered as a cover-up of his biological condition. Instead, DNA testing has confirmed that the nineteen-year-old king died quickly as a result of infection following broken bone injuries and a weakened immune system due to malaria tropica. The study of the actual mummy of Tutankhamun has established a number of things. A number of ribs on the right side of the body are missing, apparently as a result of a traumatic injury such as might result from a high-speed chariot accident. The "floating piece of bone" observed within the boy-king's skull appears to have been a result of a rushed and sloppy mummification process and not due to a fatal blow to the back of his head. Determining a cause of death such as illness, rampant infection following injury, or a toxic substance is virtually impossible after more than 3,000 years. Likewise, the physical evidence of female-like breast development, broader hips, or other combination masculine/feminine characteristics is no longer observable and perhaps offset by confirmation of well developed male genitalia.

It was definitely not the first time that a king (pharaoh) had been killed to satisfy the ambitions of a successor. In one instance, the killing was so rampant that one heir to the throne lasted only a few days and another for only a few hours. Outside the Temple of Edfu a large statue of an angry Horus, the protector god, stands in abject frustration over the rapid, multiple assassination of pharaohs. Cartouches, stylized borders used only for pharaonic names on carved walls and pillars, became smaller and smaller and were often left blank because it was not known who the next pharaoh would be or how long he might reign. Obvious signs of a monarchy in distress.

Tutankhamun was thrust into the position of being a king at the very immature age of nine or ten years and was soon renamed from Tutankhaten to Tutankhamun to reflect the total rejection of the omniscient god, Aten, and to restore the full pantheon of Egyptian gods headed by the all-powerful sun god, Amun. The actual adult in power was the boy-king's maternal great uncle, Aye, the son of Joseph (Yuya). It was Aye who controlled the military power at the new capital in Egypt and the one who had prevented Egypt's deterioration into civil war, anarchy, or complete overthrow of the monarchy. This aging and portly grand vizier to Tutankhamun had continuously been a very high-ranking member of the royal family and was not a likely assassin of the boy-king due to political ambitions of his own. Aye had already demonstrated his loyalty and ability to defend Akhenaten and Nefertiti against tremendous pressures to end their heretical reign until the pressure was simply too great to prevent a massive revolution and possible end of the monarchy. Aye would have been the principal decision-maker in facilitating the move of Egypt's capital from the newly created capital city of Tell el-Amarna to the old capital of Thebes back across to the eastern banks of the Nile. He was the one to coordinate with the hierarchy of up to 5,000 priests to re-establish all of the former gods and religious traditions and to ease out or remove Akhenaten from power. Likewise, the mysterious and temporary co-regent, Semenkhkare, Akhenaten's nephew, cousin, or half-brother, had to be abruptly removed from a divinely sanctioned position by someone's orders. The potential sole survivor for a brief period was Nefertiti, who had assumed a virtual co-equal role with her repudiated husband/king, but soon or immediately failed in her bid to hold on to power.

Discovery of King Tutankhamun's Mostly Intact Tomb

On November 22, 1922, Howard Carter was the first man to view the insides of Tutankhamun's tomb in more than three thousand years. Tutankhamun's well-concealed and very small tomb within the Valley of the Kings was found almost perfectly intact. Extensive evaluation of Tutankhamun's mummy helps to establish that he died soon after breaking his leg, as a result of infections. The smashed pieces of one or more chariots in Tutankhamun's tomb also suggest that the unanticipated death was the result of an accident and not a political/religious assassination. The accident may have occurred as the young king was being transported by chariot during his observation of war efforts being conducted in the northern region of Kadesh. The complexity of his orthopedic disabilities does suggest that Tutankhamun was more likely an observer/commander, not a virulent warrior/king leading his troops into battle.

Egyptian Hybrid Along Neva River, St. Petersburg, Russia

14
The Rush to End Monotheism in Ancient Egypt

In an unanticipated power play, Tutankhamun's Grand Vizier, Aye (Kheperkheprure Aye) maneuvered himself into the position of pharaoh following the abrupt death of the adolescent boy-king. To survive, Aye furthered a radical reversal of Akhenaten's heretical solitary god religion (Aten) and restored the ancient Egyptian gods and goddesses of the Amun religion. The accelerated and often bloody process began with the removal of Akhenaten and Aye's imposition of total authority as a regent for the nine-to ten-year-old boy-king. Prior to Aye's personal reign of four years and one month (1325 BCE – 1321 BCE), it was understood that Tutankhamun's Chief of the Armies, Horemheb, would succeed the boy-king. The succession appears to have been handled badly because both Aye and Horemheb were far older than King Tut and neither man was expected to outlive the boy-king. Also, Horemheb was either a commoner by birth or the son of a low-ranking noble family who had excelled as a soldier, then as a statesman, and finally as a diplomat during the final years of Akhenaten's reign (c.1351 BCE – 1334 BCE). Horemheb and Aye had successfully defended Akhenaten against a mounting civil war over the pharaoh's rejection of thousands of years of ancient Egyptian religion. Once that pressure was too great, however, it fully appears that Horemheb sided with the priesthood and conservative elements of Egyptian society who insisted on restoration of the Amun religion. An inevitable overthrow of the monarchy was averted by ruthless efforts to stamp out the monotheist religion of the Aten, probable assassination of the pharaoh, and manipulation of a 10-year old boy-king whose name was changed from Tutankhaten to Tutankhamun. The wily old general of the armies thus altered his political position completely and waited for his opportunity to become the reigning pharaoh. In part, he did so by marrying Nefertiti's sister and taking her as his chief wife and consort, Queen Mutnedjmet.

In the reactionary and very bloody revolt that abruptly brought down the heretic pharaoh Akhenaten and his beautiful heretic queen, Nefertiti, the immediate destruction of their new capital city of Akhetaten was begun. Block by block the west bank city built in haste to rival Thebes was disassembled and typically moved to the east bank of the Nile River for construction to honor the ancient religion of Amun. A very systematic effort, in fact, was instituted by Horemheb, known as the Oppressor Pharaoh, when he came into power just over four years later. He actually ordered the elimination of the cartouches and other records of what he considered the Amarna kings Akhenaten, Semenkhkare, Tutankhamun, and Aye. The old general of the armies, who did not leave any heirs, imposed what has been described as a "Great Edict" to re-establish the old order and specific sets of laws intended to eradicate all traces of the heretic religion. Violators of these new edicts and laws often received harsh punishments such as amputation of their nose. The sacred old religion of Amun was resurrected with a vengeance during the approximately twenty-seven-year reign of the old general of the armies, Horemheb (1321 BCE – 1292 BCE). He was the last king of the Eighteenth Dynasty and before he died in 1290 BCE, he appointed another old general of common birth Rameses I (1292 BCE – 1290 BCE), to be his successor. Horemheb did all in his power to destroy the memory of Akhenaten but did not take out his vengeance on the boy-king, Tutankhamun. The Oppressor Pharaoh was buried in the Valley of the Kings in KV57. He is portrayed by Victor Mature in the 1954 film, *The Egyptians*.

Horemheb, the Oppressor Pharaoh

Horemheb was a tough old military commander of humble birth who became a powerful Egyptian pharaoh. He was also in one of the most unique positions in world history to observe and capitalize on the sudden transition from ancient gods and goddesses to a single god and then the violent transition back to the old gods within his lifetime. Although relatively little is known about the early years of this last pharaoh of the Eighteenth Dynasty, it can be reasonably accepted that he had extensive exposure to the pharaonic court during ancient Egypt's most tumultuous period of religious metamorphosis. His military and later diplomatic career spanned the final years of Amenhotep III, a powerful pharaoh with traditional connections to the ancient gods and possible leanings toward the new sun god, Aten. Horemheb served the pharaonic court during the disastrous reign of the heretic king, Amenhotep IV (later changed to Akhenaten), as his general of the Egyptian armies north and south. As a powerful national figure during a time of extreme religious and political upheaval, Horemheb maneuvered himself into the immediate heir-apparent position to succeed the boy-king, Tutankhamun. However, in his role as the military commander stationed at the northern frontier of Egypt near Kadesh (present-day Syria), his claim to the throne was usurped by the boy-king's elderly maternal great uncle, Aye, following Tut's unanticipated death at the age of nineteen years. Horemheb was therefore in a key position to personally observe the internal workings of a failed monarchy and unprecedented upheavals bordering on civil war. As a senior military officer of great authority and non-royal background, he had access to firsthand information that was likely unimaginable in the populace, who had long believed in the infallibility and divinity of their king. Horemheb was able to observe, experience, and personally benefit from extreme radical transitions of religion and politics that led him from a humble birth to death as a pharaonic divine/king.

Although rising through the ranks to be general of the armies during the reigns of Akhenaten, Tutankhamun, and Aye, Horemheb was likely humbled by his origins as a commoner. Still, he would have recognized that he was free of the genetic abnormalities that were so apparent within the inbred royal family of Akhenaten, his wife and half-sister, Nefertiti, and their son, Tutankhamun. The rudely deposed heretic king, Akhenaten, may have been impotent, or sterile, and was riddled with physiological defects typical of excessive royal inbreeding. Exposure to the day-to-day affairs of the Egyptian monarchy in a variety of positions, including appointment as Tutankhamun's deputy (equivalent to a crown prince in the absence of a legitimate male heir) likewise must have contributed to Horemheb's confidence for plotting his way into the position of pharaoh of both Upper and Lower Egypt. His firsthand knowledge of the vulnerabilities and corruption within the royal palaces gave him the opportunities to outlast and replace first Vizier Aye and then Pharaoh Aye by one means or another, including possible violent means. His roughly 27-year rule as pharaoh was marked with the implementation of harsh laws to stem corruption at all levels. Possibly the virtual non-violation of Tutanhkamun's tomb was due to Horemheb's aggressive, militaristic efforts to control the systematic corruption at all levels of Egyptian society that had turned tomb robbing into a broad-based industry and showed disrespect for the deceased pharaoh's afterlife and relationship to the gods. Along with Horemheb's new code of justice were harsh penalties that could range from restitution to expulsion to having the nose of the perpetrator cut off. Also, Horemheb went to great lengths to justify his right to occupy the position of pharaoh by reinforcing the restoration of all of the old gods, the priesthood, and by linking himself to royalty by marrying the sister of the displaced Queen Nefertiti. In addition, he linked himself to the old gods by emphasizing his connection with the powerful god, Horus, who was the patron of the town of Horemheb's birthplace and the god he was named after. His name, Horemheb Meryamun, can be interpreted as "Horus is in Jubilation, Beloved of Amun." His first wife had died prior to his ascending to the throne. As pharaoh, he made Mutnedjmet his chief wife and queen. She was a younger sister of Nefertiti but may have been the daughter of his rival for the throne, the elderly pharaoh Aye.

Horemheb was not successful in stamping out corruption in spite of his introduction of many military officers to positions of authority within the government, priesthood, and judicial system. The incentive for personal gain was simply too great and too long entrenched. With such a militaristic and authoritarian effort to deal with widespread corruption, he was known as the Oppressor Pharaoh. He made special efforts as well to eradicate the historical record of the four prior kings of the Armana Period Akhenaten, Smenkhkare, Tutankhamun, and Aye. He died in 1290 BCE and his elaborate tomb in the Valley of the Kings is known as KV57. Tutanhkamun's very small tomb, probably intended for Aye before he became a pharaoh, is known as KV62. Tomb KV56 is known as the Gold Tomb and was apparently the burial site of a royal child whose identity remains unknown. The mystery of KV55 is that it was the apparent dumping ground of much of Akhenaten's reign and was intended to be dismissed and forgotten in Horemheb's systematic efforts to erase all memory and traces of the Armana kings. To prevent a possible coup d'etat during his long reign, he divided the Egyptian army into northern and southern sectors. Also, prior to his death as an elderly pharaoh, Horemheb appointed his own vizier, a former military commander like himself, as his successor. Ancient Egyptian history recognizes that appointee as Pa-Rameses. Like Horemheb, he was an elderly pharaoh of all of Egypt without royal blood. He shortened his name to Rameses I and was the founder of a new dynasty that reigned during the most successful period in Egyptian history. It was a time when the pharaoh would become synonymous with divinity in the case of his grandson, Rameses the Great (Rameses II).

Thus Horemheb will always be remembered as the last king of the Eighteenth Dynasty and clearly a successful military leader and survivor of the radical religious upheaval of ancient Egypt that transitioned from thousands of years of pagan beliefs to little more than a dozen years of monotheism followed by violent return to the long-established paganism. Among Horemheb's accomplishments was the restoration of the old temples and reinstatement of the extensive hierarchy of the priesthood, which had so aligned itself with the long succession of pharaohs. Ironically, the systematic destruction and desecration of Akhenaten's new religion and new temple city to use the building blocks for other projects has done the most to preserve stone carvings now over 3,000 years old that were faced inward in construction projects now severely weathered by time. His military prowess in the field helped to sustain Egypt during the reign of the radical heretic king, Akhenaten, and allowed him to amass his own political stock during a time when the major cracks in the monarchy that often considered itself divine were so apparent to the insiders who were familiar with the uses and abuses of real power. As the heir apparent to Tutankhamun he may have exercised diplomatic roles to gain even more insight on the inner workings of the monarchy and certainly felt betrayed following the sudden and controversial death of the boy-king that his rightful position was usurped by an elderly power-player who was even more familiar with the mystique and realities of a monarchy with divine connections.

Comparative Ancient Gods					
	Canaanite	Roman	Greek	Egyptian	Mesopotamian
Paternal god	El	Saturn	Cronos	Amun-Ra	Anu
Maternal god	Athirat	Juno	Hera	Mut	Antu
Earth god	El, Yahweh	Jupiter	Zeus	Set	Enlil
Earth god	Athirat	Minerva	Athena	Isis	Ninhursag
Creator	Baal	Vulcan	Apollo	Osiris	Enki
War god	Anat	Mars	Ares	Horus	Marduk
Underworld	Mot	Pluto	Hades	Anubis	Nergal
Love god	Isaalat	Venus	Aphrodite	Hathor	Asherah
Messenger	————	Mercury	Hermes	Thoth	Ninurta

Resurrected gods included Attis, Adonis, Gilgamesh, and Osiris
Joseph Campbell, *The Power of Myth*, NY Doubleday, 1988, p. 179

Stonehenge c. 2500 BCE

15
Historical Transcendence to a Universal God

Early Transition from Paganism to a Solitary Regional God

The fragmented historical record of ancient times does suggest that in Egypt and in Mesopotamia there had been movements to consolidate and reduce the variety of gods and supernatural spirits that impacted the daily lives of what might be considered ordinary citizens and the hierarchy they lived within. Dissatisfactions with the complexities and vagaries of excess numbers of competing gods, goddesses, and spirits led to a tendency for different regions to choose a personal god as the divine force most likely to represent them at times of crisis and conflict with their world. Great focus likely remained on efforts to please that specific god or smaller group of gods by ritualistic methods for which there was some consensus and former history. Animal sacrifice would have been common, symbolic, and graphic as well. Human sacrifice was more inclined to become rare.

Throughout the ancient world of Mesopotamia and Egypt there had long been ingrained histories of having multiple gods for different purposes and unique powers, especially the generalized power to alleviate suffering and to provide protection against external threats such as floods, crop failures, storm damage, diseases, drought, famine, and lethal marauders. Each major settlement was inclined to identify with a smaller number of gods and goddesses as personal guardians who provided various protections to their clan or region. It was on that basis and around the period of 2000 to 1800 BCE that an extraordinary man named

Abram (later renamed Abraham), living in the Mesopotamian city of Ur, accepted the spiritual directive of his personal god to leave his father, a pagan idol maker, and resettle in the land of Canaan near the Mediterranean coast. The purpose of the relocation was to cast out all other gods and for his descendants and followers to accept the one true living God. In biblical time, however, Abraham is described as living to the age of 175 years and of being 75 years of age before he marries Sarai (later renamed Sarah) in the city of Haran in northwestern Mesopotamia. The reality of paganism throughout the remainder of the region was not denied, and only the rudimentary elements of a regional monotheism began to take root. It would be many centuries later that paganism would begin to lose its fervor and a more universal monotheism would take its place.

In experiencing a direct relationship and personal communication with his god, he followed the divine commands as he understood them without question. In doing so he broke with the polytheist traditions of his native land and reduced the pantheon of gods that his peers accepted to a single divine force. This God, who communicated directly with select humans, acknowledged no other gods but was aligned with only select individuals, not a universal God as he was later perceived to be. It was not until the time of Moses, however, that God gave the Israelites permission to address Him as "Yahweh."

The Patriarchs

Appearing to have Semitic rather than Sumerian origins, Abraham, Isaac (only son of Abraham and Sarah), and Abraham's grandson, Jacob, are collectively known as the Patriarchs. Isaac's son, Jacob, was later renamed Israel and his descendants are considered the Israelites. Jews, however, are originally descended from Judah, who was one of Jacob's twelve sons. The older term, "Hebrews" may refer to descendants of Eber, the son of Shem, and the grandson of Noah. Thus descendants of Eber have been described as Shemites, but not Jews, or Israelites. For practical purposes, the terms "Hebrews" and "Israelites" are older terms for the group that we now call Jews, who are of Semitic origin. In the Bible, the term "Hebrew" is first used of Abraham, and the term "Israelites" naturally starts with Jacob and Israel. The descendants of Abraham's first son, Ishmael, by his second wife, Hagar, have been referred to as Ishmaelites, but it was several thousand years later that the association with the Muslim religion, not an ethnic one, was made at the time of Muhammad.

The radical break in religious belief from paganism to adherence to a solitary living god eventually manifested itself in the formation of a tenacious minority among the Canaanite/Mesopotamian people. The descendants of Jacob identified themselves as Israelite tribes. These mostly nomadic tribes set themselves apart from their linguistic and ethnic cousins in Canaan for many generations up to and beyond the time of Moses and Joshua in approximately 1600 BCE. The decisive difference over belief in a living god versus the old pagan ways made the Israelite tribes a fiercely cohesive minority within the land of Canaan. With military successes to his credit, increasing numbers of people were willing to accept the power and presence of Abraham and his personal god. The tenacity of the people who accepted this monotheistic religion was a decisive factor in keeping them together through great adversities. The Israelite tribes, as they later called themselves, even survived the tendency of some of the followers of Moses to drift back to idolatrous other gods. For some people there may always be the uncertainty of the actual decade or even century that Moses led his people out of Egypt.

The eruption of the island of Thera (Santorini) places that time at roughly 1600 BCE and makes Moses the most significant driving force in maintaining the monotheistic religion of Abraham, Isaac, and Jacob. Some scholars may cling to the notion that an Egyptian pharaoh by the name of Akhenaten transformed himself into Moses or was contemporaneous with Moses around the time of 1333 BCE. The coincidental factors in both men's lives are stunning but hardly enough to convince most people that the two men were one and the same when making comparisons of biblical descriptions with the massive eruption of the Minoan island of Thera.

History of God

In her book, *A History of God*, Karen Armstrong has acknowledged that the perception of God has changed many times. As far back as 100,000 years and more, humans have sought explanations for all of the apparent chaos, conflict, disease, and evil experienced within their own lives. The miracle of birth and the devastation of death seemed to have an immediate parallel in the rising and setting (birth and death) of the sun each and every day. All of the other complexities of who, what, where, when, why, and how deserved an answer, no matter how crude and misinformed, and the surviving answers, passed along in oral traditions, were likely to take on a sacred and unchallengeable aura. The solution to such far-reaching questions was typically the creation of a pagan god(s) story that was filled with imagination, yet described something of a superhero with humanoid characteristics. The specific god or goddess could be a source of a close, perhaps warm, personal relationship, and still be viewed mostly in the abstract. The unexplainable was given an answer. The local gods were relevant for a particular region and could potentially come into conflict with the gods of another region.

Small children could be given answers that genuinely seemed to be beyond the personal opinion of the parent, which would justify taking a particular course of action rather than confronting the parent or simply doing things at random.

The early Abraham, the eventual patriarch of Judaism, Christianity, and Islam, wrestled with pagan issues as well. He was caught up in a regionalized world where ritual sacrifice was still an essential part of the communication with god or gods. It was still possible to experience a conversation, have an argument, or even share food with a god. Abraham was "put to the test" when his living god asked him to sacrifice his own son but later allowed the ritual sacrifice of a ram or goat as sufficient proof of his love and faith. It would be many more centuries before the Israelite living god would become the universal god of a vast majority of the world's people.

Reconciling Religious and Historical Dates

Calculating reasonable dates for events mentioned in the Old Testament has consistently been difficult because much of the text was committed to writing as much as 500 to 1,000 years after the fact, the actual writers are not identified, and few, if any, individuals would have been keeping records in the form of an objective historical text. Instead, a good bit of literary license and leaps of faith are placed alongside dated pottery shards, carved stone stelae, the occasional tomb, hieroglyphics, bits of DNA, carbon-14 dating, Dead Sea scrolls, and many bits of cultural cross-referencing. At some vague time, for example, a great famine struck portions of Canaan, and Jacob, the last of the great biblical patriarchs, gathered his family and followers and immigrated across the southern border to Egypt. The Egyptian record does not take note of a mass influx of Semitic people and does not pinpoint the historical date. Instead, as in most dominant cultures throughout history, impoverished immigrants were probably exploited as cheap labor, not as slaves. It would have been too easy in that instance for small numbers of Semitic people to pass to and from the Egyptian border at will to be forcefully held in slavery. Instead, it was acknowledged that the Israelites prospered and their numbers grew. The solidarity of their religious beliefs would have been at odds with the dominant Egyptian culture and likely blocked assimilation and dispersal outside of the Goshen area of the Nile Delta. The time came, however (date still imprecise), when the population and staunch religion of the Israelites in Goshen could represent a threat to a weak pharaonic government that was being pressured by Upper (southern) Egypt as well. The probability that the Israelites had occupied Goshen for a period of four hundred years seems unlikely. Such an extended period of time has more likely been cited to reconcile the belief that the Exodus occurred around 1250 BCE, not 1600 BCE. The historic clock of chronological reality, however, is reset by specific dating of the massive eruption of the island of Thera, which very specifically dates and reconfirms events described leading up to the mass exodus of the Israelites out of northeastern Egypt. Thus, the failure to ever document the name of the reigning pharaoh at the actual time of the Exodus and the absence of Egyptian confirmation of the dramatically tragic event may well be a function of the event occurring 500 or 600 years prior to being committed to a surviving written form. It is improbable that the date of the Exodus coincided with the reign of Akhenaten, or the later reign of Rameses II, because the historical record for each king was far too prominent for such an omission to occur.

A classic example of hyperbole relates to King Solomon, the son of King David, who was born near the year of 1,035 BCE and ascended to the throne of Israel around the year of 1,018 BCE. He is reported to have had as many as 700 wives and perhaps as many as 300 concubines during his lifetime. Such was the exaggerated foreign policy plan of a resourceful monarch. Many of his relationships were made as extensions of binding and favorable relationships with bordering kingdoms and ethnic groups. One of the most notable of those controversial relationships was the marriage to an Ethiopian sovereign by the name of Sheba (Magda). She was pregnant when she departed from the royal court of King Solomon in Jerusalem and returned to Ethiopia. The resulting child, David, ultimately matured and became the first king or Jewish emperor of Ethiopia and ruled under the name of Menelik I. He also introduced monotheism to that region and his religious influences in Ethiopia are remembered to this date.

The Solitary God of Zarathustra

Another theory about the origin of monotheism refers to a movement in the border region between present-day Iran and Afghanistan, which was led by a dynamic prophet beginning around 1,000 BCE by the name of Zarathustra (Zoroaster in Greek). He referred to the solitary god of his people as Ahura Mazda. The focus of their religion tended to be a variant in the struggle between good and evil and emphasized universal truthfulness, justice, and goodness as a means of overcoming the adversities of evil. The Zoroastrian god is viewed as one of the first universal gods, and not the god of a specific group of people. This fairly isolated movement has continued to this date and has evolved with time but has been largely suppressed by conflicts with Islam.

Mithras

The ancient pagan/religious cult of Mithras has been associated with the Persian (Iranian) god, Mithra, and may have Indo-European origins tracing back several thousand years before the birth of Jesus Christ. The definitive study for many decades was written by the Belgian archaeologist and historian, Franz Cumont (1868-1947), in his book, *The Mysteries of Mithra*. More recent opinions suggest that the ardent and secretive followers of Mithras were more likely of Greco-Roman descent who borrowed little more than the ancient god's name and instead focused on a pagan astrological cult that gave major credence to the symbolism of the bull (Taurus), the equinoxes, solstices, and the mysteries of the universe (heaven). This cult was quite active at the time of Jesus Christ and for several centuries afterward and had great influence on the early development of Christianity. There were literally hundreds of small temples throughout the Roman Empire that were often located underground and restricted to male-only membership. The greatest concentration of temples was in the city of Rome. The followers of Mithras were especially active in the region now occupied by the Vatican.

Parallels between the cult of Mithras and early Christianity are much too numerous to have occurred by chance. Both Mithra and Jesus Christ were born following the union of a deity and a human on the 25th of December. Both emphasized mankind's possibility for redemption, asceticism, baptism, charity toward others, and resurrection through sacrifice. Both considered Sunday to be sacred and emphasized a future judgment day to determine each deceased person's immortality in either heaven or hell. Both Mithra and Jesus Christ ascended to heaven near the time of the vernal equinox.

16
Israelite Prophets and Prophecy

During the ninth century BCE the prophet Elijah challenged the Canaanites' belief in the pagan god Baal to end a severe drought and famine that was plaguing the region. Baal was considered to be a creator god and the Canaanite god of storms, but when the challenge failed to bring relief to the area, Elijah used trickery to gather 450 priests of Baal in one location and brought fire down from the sky and had the priests slaughtered. The prophet then fled to Mt. Horeb where he saw a vision of God. The vision appeared during a dead calm, not a time of raging storm, fire and earthquake, but in a barely audible voice. The fabled challenge was just one more revelation that the living God was omniscient yet not subject to definition, or within the grasp of the human imagination. In extreme contrast, Isaiah reported a terrifying contact with God who appeared to be sitting on a throne.

In the approximate period from 605 to 597 BCE, the Babylonian Empire to the east sustained invasions of Judah and imposed the first wave of deportations of select Israelite people eastward to the Babylonian Empire. Over a period of time, at least three different waves of Israelite captives were forced into labor and other positions of value to the Empire. A major second wave of captivity and exile began in 597 BCE, and a third wave occurred in 586 BCE that was lead by Nebuchadnezzar II. It was not until 539/538 BCE that the Babylonian Empire was overthrown by the Persian Empire under Cyrus II (Cyrus the Great). It was also at that time that Cyrus II allowed the captive Jews to return to their homeland and facilitated the rebuilding of their temple. Among the twists of irony for that transitional period was the capture of the 10 northern Israelite tribes from the Kingdom of Judah and the scattering to the winds of those "lost tribes." Then, upon the return of the Jewish captives, who adhered to strict interpretations of their faith during the captivity period of up to 70 years, it was discovered that pagan and other influences had taken hold. The captivity and subsequent return were therefore pivotal in reinforcing strict interpretations of the Jewish faith and the relationship with their living God, Yahweh. What followed were potentially life-and-death confrontations with the blended and altered beliefs of non-exiled Jews, pagan worshippers, and mixed ethnicity immigrants who no longer had the same tenaciously held belief in Judaism and a single living God. The Judeans in particular clung to their regional God and the Samaritans held to their own version of Judaism which they believed was the true version. Thus, during that period of Babylonian captivity, a prominent prophet known as Second Isaiah sought to convince people that the God of the Jewish people was a God of all nations.

Much of Second Isaiah's early writings survived the ravages of time and has been confirmed by the Dead Sea Scrolls. He prophesied a dismal future for all residents of Judea who did not accept the true living God of Abraham. He also predicted the restoration and unification of Israel as an independent nation, which would not be the case for more than 2,500 years. His prolific writings also provided some references to a coming messiah who would have a connection to the House of King David, who would convey the glories of God's kingdom, and of life after death. Debate continues about the possibility that the books of Second Isaiah were written and perhaps re-written by more than one author over an extended period of time. His writings are not exclusively confined to the Babylonian Exile period and appear to make special efforts to condemn idolaters and to describe

God as a universal God of all nations, not simply of the Chosen People. Second Isaiah's prophesies were widely disseminated among the Jewish people and may account for a major impact upon Jesus Christ's ministry. For example, when disciples of John the Baptist asked of Jesus, "Are you the one who is come, or are we to wait for another?" Jesus replied, "Go and tell John what you have seen and heard the blind regain their sight, the lame walk, lepers are cleansed, the deaf hear, the dead are raised, the poor have the good news proclaimed to them." (Luke: 7 20-22).

There has long been a history of regional prophets whose concerns and effectiveness were confined to limited areas. It was almost 600 years before another major prophet appeared. He was from the region of Galilee and was born into a rural area of the Israelite world at the time of its occupation by the armies and magistrates of Rome. The region was ruled with extreme harshness in a very overt effort to suppress any rebellion in the subjugated territories. Crucifixion was therefore just one of the intentionally inhumane methods of punishment for select criminal activities or transgressions against the authority of Rome. The intent, without any hint of remorse, was to be an absolute deterrent to the masses. Approximately one generation prior to the birth of Jesus Christ, at least 6,000 rebellious slaves lead by Spartacus had been executed by crucifixion along the southern peninsula of Italy by the vindictive army of Roman Emperor Crassus. After Jesus was himself crucified for perceived sedition against Rome, more and more Jews and gentiles shared the belief that he was a messiah. Jesus was not known to have committed anything to writing that has survived and he did not specifically say he was the son of God. Instead he referred to his father in heaven. The Lord's Prayer, referring to everyone, begins with: "Our father...." Early Christians, in fact, did not consider Jesus Christ (from the Greek word "Christos" that literally means "the anointed one,") to be divine but rather as having a special relationship with God. It was Paul (Saul), in particular, who incessantly took the word of Jesus to others within the Roman Empire, a pagan empire, to convince them that Jesus was the "redeemer of the world," yet Paul had no direct contact with Jesus. It was Paul who also discouraged single adults from marriage because he sincerely believed the "end times" were coming soon.

The Talmud

The Talmud is an ancient text of rabbinic principles and writings that interpret and explain the Torah scriptures. It is an influential text on the everyday conduct of Jewish life and draws heavily on the Old Testament. The time-honored written text is a composite of Judaism's challenges, questions, riddles, and even contradictions. The structure of the text, beginning with ancient scrolls, is analytical and a depository that contains myths and history in addition to religious philosophy and doctrine. The origins of the Talmud date back to the period of Israelite captivity by the Babylonian Empire, circa 586 BCE. It includes much oral tradition of the Jewish people prior to that time. The text places great emphasis on stories associated with Moses and other prophets throughout Jewish history. The Talmud is interconnected with the Torah, and helps to make the Talmud less of an enigma and more of an instructional, analytical text. The Talmud includes many philosophical questions, logic, reasoning, science, and even humor. It is the surviving document of efforts to annihilate Judaism dating back to the Roman destruction of Jerusalem in 70 CE. It is also a book that covers virtually all aspects of Jewish life and seeks to summarize the laws and customs of the Jewish people. The original language of the Talmud was Hebrew, which in ancient times was written without vowels until approximately 1,000 CE, and can be difficult to accurately interpret. The text was later translated into many languages, including Aramaic, Greek, and most of the contemporary languages of the world. In brief, the Talmud is an evolving history and collection of philosophical statements in reference to the Jewish people. The continuity of this complex and growing document is in various ways comparable to the religious cultures of the ancient Egyptians and religions of the Near East and Far East.

The forced emigration of people of the Jewish faith to other countries around the world has served to broaden and expand the Talmud. Even during the Middle Ages, when the text was declared blasphemist and systematic efforts to torch all copies were imposed by the administration of Pope Gregory IX, the precious book survived. The first printed copy of the Talmud appeared in Venice in 1519, a time of continued inquisition in Europe. The European purges continued erratically for centuries and reached a most extreme hysteria and murderous conflict under the authoritarian dictatorship of the Nazi Party. Judaism has consistently prevailed and gained strength while facing extreme adversity such as in the process of tempering metal with flame followed by rapid cooling. The longevity of Judaism is reflected in the Talmud, which contains a reverence for the wisdom and intelligence of the ancients as well as those living in the present. In short, it is a religious book of hope and identity. The Talmud is representative of the dedicated faith that was the first to withstand the great pressures of the pagan world and gained strength as the faithful were dispersed throughout the globe for nearly two millennia (Diaspora). The State of Israel, founded in 1948 after World War II, has repeatedly demonstrated the desire and capability to survive and grow in a region that continues to be assaulted by much international pressure and hostility. Now, however, the exodus from much of the Holy Land has been predominantly of the Arab Christian faithful. The June, 2009, issue of National Geographic documents a major decline in the Arab Christian population of the Eastern Mediterranean, which represents less than nine percent of the total population by the end of 2007.

Jewish Disapora

17
The Divinity of Jesus Christ

The divinity of Jesus Christ has typically not been questioned for a very long time among Christians. It is faith in the combined message of redemption and resurrection, beginning with a focus on "the least among us," that has preserved the image of Jesus Christ as a Jewish messiah and Son of God. The promise of an afterworld without intimidation, pain, or fear was all the enticement needed for people living under the heel of the Roman boot and a world that often contained many of the worst imaginable abuses and suffering. Consider the paraphrased comment by Christ that it was easier for a camel to get through the eye of a needle than for a rich man to get into heaven. The image may appear improbable but did not preclude the rich from getting into heaven. First, the eye of a needle was not a description of a sewing implement. It was a metaphor for the small gates or openings in the protective walls of cities. The purpose was to prevent armed raiders from riding into a city in large numbers and at a high speed. Instead, a camel and rider could pass through the low and narrow opening only one at a time, slowly, and with some difficulty, but not be precluded from entry. Second, it was Christ's focus on rural, ordinary people, especially women and children, rather than the rich and powerful of the urban areas that endeared so many people to his new faith. With rural origins and overt hostility toward the greedy money lenders and power brokers who were so conspicuous in the urban temples, it is very consistent that Jesus Christ did not seek personal wealth and did not endorse enormous temples gilded in gold or confiscations of wealth from people of other religious beliefs. "Let he who is without sin cast the first stone" was a re-examination of the top-down justice system that was filled with inequities and dominated by the rich and powerful. The messages of turning the other cheek and loving one's neighbor were metaphors for acquiring survival skills at a time when the Jewish people could have been totally annihilated by the Roman Empire. The messages of Jesus Christ were conveyed orally within the three-year period of his ministry and have had a lasting impact on much of humanity. Still, it was not for many decades after the death and resurrection of Christ that his words and actions were committed to writing by others.

Like Moses, Akhenaten, and other deity or virtual-deity figures throughout history, the early childhood of Jesus Christ is mostly unknown and a major mystery. The absence of detail is especially profound for a man whose birth was accompanied by angels, a special guiding star, wise men bearing gifts suitable for an important monarch, and the quest for a messiah who would prevail against the detested Roman occupiers. At what other time and place in history would such an individual be completely transparent, be home schooled without any record of the influences, and then appear on the world's stage at the approximate age of 30 years? Was the message, the gospel, of his ministry not enough? Much is still unknown about the one man who has been studied, revered, and at times questioned for a full two thousand years. He appears to have shared many of the beliefs and values of the Judaic subgroup known as the Essenes, espoused rural values, and spoke Aramaic, yet he left no personally written trace of his ministry, and the Aramaic language has virtually ceased to exist, except among some Syrian Christians and scholars of that language.

The context of the times in which Jesus lived is critical for a broader understanding of one of the most revered humans to ever set foot on this planet. Jesus of Nazareth was born into a rural community about 65 miles from Jerusalem if one were able to travel in a straight line. Travel was mostly by foot over rough-hewn trails that had as much to do with animal grazing as they did from moving from place to place. Travel was likely scrutinized closely during the time that the Israelite people were under the detested occupation of Roman authorities and the Roman army. The Roman Empire was near the peak of its absolute power and had extended its influence throughout Northern Africa and much of present-day Europe. The empire was obsessed with control issues in all of its colonial possessions and did not hesitate to use the most extreme and publicly heinous forms of punishment to demonstrate that control to the masses. In return, the Roman Empire of that time was relatively tolerant of religious and spiritual beliefs that were not in conflict with the hodgepodge of pagan beliefs that had been absorbed from their various colonies.

The Romans had used crucifixion as a method of execution for at least 70 years prior to the crucifixion of Jesus Christ. An historian of the times recorded that approximately 40 years prior to the birth of Jesus, as many as 2,000 people were crucified in a single day for the entertainment of Roman politician and general Quintilius Varus who served under Emperor Augustus. He was notable to the historic record for his famous for his plea, "Give me back my legions" after Germanic tribes ambushed and slaughtered 25,000 Roman legionnaires. Also, following the sack of Jerusalem in 70 CE, the Romans crucified as many as 500 people in a single day. It was commonplace for the time to crucify persons accused of certain crimes, runaway or disobedient slaves, captured prisoners of war, and perceived threats to Roman authority since it was the most cruel, visible, and severe deterrent that could be imagined. Little doubt would have existed about the consequences for challenging Rome's authority. Execution, imprisonment, and even forced relocation combined with enslavement were sufficiently commonplace to attract little notice except for those involved and their families. The ultimate abomination for the Israelite people, however, was the conflict between paganism and monotheism, which had no tolerance for graven images or other gods in addition to the one living God. There was resentment that the Jewish hierarchy of the priesthood had become overly accommodating with Rome just to survive. As a result, there was a splintering of religious beliefs and intensification of the expectation that a divinely appointed messiah would free the Jewish faithful from the oppressive yoke of Roman occupation and authority. The most enduring and successful of these periodic messiahs was Jesus of Nazareth. But for many contemporaries there was disappointment that "the Prince of Peace" advocated a non-violent approach to the hated Romans to avoid annihilation as a religiously devout population and to instead find peace in another world after death.

The Middle East of ancient times had long had plagues, diseases, wars, and natural disasters on massive scales. The tendency had long been to attribute illnesses, disabling conditions, and premature deaths to the intervention of gods or evil spirits. There was very high infant mortality and perhaps as many as half of the people did not live beyond the age of five years. Overall life spans were short, existence was a grinding ordeal except for the privileged few, and it was common for people to look with great favor and skepticism on anyone who seemed to possess the power of healing or ability to make miracles happen. Such individuals were greatly revered for the immediate good they could do and subject to brutal execution or banishment if they proved to be a false prophet or fake healer. It was Jesus' willingness to approach and to give hope and perhaps actual healing to outcast lepers that was among the first of his many miracles. The very first miracle was in turning water to wine at a wedding in Cana of Galilee. Subsequent medical miracles such as raising Lazarus from the dead quickly contributed to his reputation as an extraordinary healer if not a representative of God. He was also a man who appealed to ordinary people's deep felt needs for food, water, good health, and uplifting ideals for surviving in a harsh world. His teachings and wonder workings stirred up strong feelings among the countryside's rural poor and dispossessed. His physical appearance would have been typical of his time and place. The rigors of a subsistence life tended to produce lean, hardy individuals with a Mediterranean complexion, dark hair and eyes typical of Jewish males in the first century. Beard and hair length was kept short to minimize the discomfort of lice and infrequent bathing. It is quite probable that he would blend in with his peers in rural settings of the times. Ironically, most painted images of Jesus Christ from the Middle Ages onward have portrayed him as mostly Aryan in appearance with long brown hair, a full beard, and perhaps a glowing halo over his head. It was the message, not the image, which has set Jesus apart for almost two thousand years.

According to the Gospels, a fervor of interest soon swelled around Jesus and he began to attract dangerously large crowds which in time would attract the unwanted attention of the Roman authorities. Of necessity, Jesus may have himself been attracted to a local group of fishermen who would soon become his disciples because he could continue to speak to small groupings of people on the shore from a small fishing boat and not be swarmed by the crush of the crowd. He was clearly a charismatic speaker with a revolutionary interest in downtrodden, ordinary people like himself. He treated mentally and physically impaired men, women, and children as if they were God's creations as well, not subordinate inferiors as was so typical of the times. He was edgy with the rich and powerful, yet he offered hope and positive alternatives to those who would listen. His three-year ministry was marked by an austere lifestyle with little income and without a desire to attain worldly possessions. His radical message for making peace with the world as it was was one of acceptance and tolerance of others rather than hate and rebellion, and the promise of a more fulfilling future life after death. Combined with the power to create miracles, the message of resurrection for even "the least among us" was intensely powerful and spawned a new religion with billions of adherents.

"I am bringing you good news of great joy for all of the people
To you is born this day a Savior, who is the Messiah, the Lord."
The Gospel according to Luke 210-11

Roman Emperor Constantine

It was not until Rome's improbable victory during the battle of Milvia in 313 CE that Emperor Constantine declared Christianity to be acceptable along with several other religions at the time. Previously, Christians had been persecuted by Roman authorities for almost three centuries and Rome was nearing collapse as an empire when Emperor Constantine placed his faith in the Christian God along with pagan gods. He was not the one, however, to declare Christianity as the state religion of the Roman Empire. It was during the year 380 that Emperor Theodosius took the position of making Christianity the official religion of the Roman Empire. During Constantine's reign, the subject of Jesus Christ's divinity was still unresolved. There had previously been ongoing debates in the city of Alexandria and other Mediterranean region cities up to the fourth century about the divinity of Christ. The fledgling Christian church of the time was split about fifty-fifty on the subject. It was not until the Council of Nicea in 325 CE that Jesus was declared fully divine. That declaration, however, invoked another raging debate about God and the son of God being two separate entities. The Nicene Creed was then promulgated to declare that there were actually three entities God, the Son of God, and the Holy Spirit (Trinity) that could be viewed as one and the same.

Prophecy and Divinity

The human condition has evolved on this unique planet over hundreds of thousands of years within biological restraints that have altered little. Birth, childhood, adolescence (if any), young adulthood, and old adulthood have been followed by death in an infinite variety of forms and without exception. This progression, based on the initial joining of two human cells (zygote), has repeated itself countless numbers of times with only the most minor of genetic mutations for up to a half-million years. In contrast, the interpretations of the meaning and purpose of our existence have been as varied as there are stars in the universe. Laws of physics, especially the law of gravity, have usually been immutable realities. We can only occupy the present moment and are impacted by the past in virtually everything we do whether we are consciously aware of it or not. Still, we cannot reliably foretell the future or mentally manipulate the future. For such extra human or superhuman tasks, we have relied on deities and to a much lesser degree to intermediaries who may be called prophets, oracles, psychics, fortune-tellers, magicians, mystics, angels, seers, visionaries, and even charlatans.

In narrowing the phenomenon of prophecy to three of the world's major faiths Judaism, Christianity, and Islam, the domain of prophecy is largely confined to the last 4,000 years. Jewish scripture, for example, has identified approximately 50 mostly male prophets of Israel beginning with the Patriarchs Abraham, Isaac, and Jacob. These divinely inspired prophets of early monotheism were deemed to be among the very first to communicate in a dialogue with the true living God. These prophets of the Old Testament publicly made assertions that they had attained private access to a true living god with unlimited powers to foretell and to influence the future. Divine messages could thus be given a human face and voice as the prophet conveyed information to those willing to listen and to adapt their behavior accordingly. These living, breathing intermediaries were possibly inspired by or selected by the deity due to their spiritual commitments and perhaps other factors. Honored and revered prophets found themselves in a position of being an insightful voice of reason between the people in their sphere of influence and the all-powerful monarchies or natural events that could so dominate or traumatize large groups of people.

Prophets were typically revered for their gifts of foretelling the future and for giving a spiritual interpretation to life's mysteries as a psychic gift from the living God. It was in the prophet's best interest, however, to not be an infallible crystal ball reader, but rather to offer suggestions on leading a spiritual and ethical life. Prophecy tends to be based on generalized parables, metaphors, analogies, and allegories, rather than definitive statements that could be taken as absolutely correct, or, heaven forbid, completely wrong. Because of mixed reactions to the outcome of virtually any traumatic situation, people within range of the prophet's words were not equally pleased with the message.

Stated another way, people will have a wide range of reactions to another person who seems to be unquestionably right too often and in an authoritarian manner that cannot be challenged. People in every group will usually argue about every subject before some degree of consensus is reached. But woe to the prophet who is clearly mistaken or mistaken too often. Such a person quickly loses all credibility and is subject to being executed or banished as a false prophet.

Most notable of the prophets of Jewish scriptures after the patriarchs were Moses, his brother Aaron, and his sister, Miriam, who accompanied her brothers throughout the Exodus. Moses has been viewed as one of the last persons to have had an actual dialogue with the living God, to have seen a fiery manifestation of God, and to convince God to take a different position on a controversial issue. The importance of Moses to Judaism, Christianity, and Islam cannot be underestimated. What is known of the early prophets, however, comes to us as oral tradition that likely dates back to 1600 BCE in the case of Moses and as much as 2000 BCE in the case of Abraham, Isaac, and Jacob. In those early times there was the real potential that detailed accounts of the early prophets were subject to varying degrees of spiritual spin to keep the focus on the Israelite people and a regionalized living God rather than openly professing to be a universal living God. The external world in those 2000 years prior to the birth of Christ was largely a pagan world that was not receptive to the reality of a universal living God. It would be the prophecies of Moses, Jesus Christ, and Muhammad, in particular, that would so radically alter the pagan world.

18
Islam

By sheer numbers alone Islam is definitely one of the world's great religions. The total numbers of Islamic (Muslim) faithful are estimated to be well over one billion people worldwide and continuing to expand at a rate slightly greater than Christianity. Christianity is the largest of the three major faiths of the Eastern Mediterranean region, and approximately one-third of the world's population identify themselves as Christians. One of the first major differences between the two, however, is that Christianity includes a far greater diversity of beliefs than Islam. Among Christians there are Roman Catholics, Eastern Orthodox, Anglican, and literally thousands of Protestant and fundamentalist denominations or groups that are recognized and continuing to evolve. Islam, by comparison, is far more conservative and, with some minor exceptions, the vast majority of Muslims belong to one of two major denominations, the Sunni (85-90%) and the Shi'a (10-15%). Muslim faithful are concentrated in the Middle East, North Africa, and large parts of Asia, including Indonesia, and can be found in almost every part of the world. The presence of Judaism and Christianity on the Arabian Peninsula, however, continues to be in a state of declining numbers.

One of the first distinctions among the three great faiths is that Islam traces its origins to Abraham and his son Ishmael by his second wife, Hagar. Both Judaism and Christianity trace their origins to Abraham and his second son, Isaac, by his first wife, Sarah. Each of the great faiths evolved from a prior period of paganism and a move from polytheism to strict monotheism. In the Muslim faith, Jesus Christ is regarded as a very important prophet, but, like Muhammad, is not considered to be an actual deity. Muhammad ibn Abdullah was born in the Arabian city of Mecca (Mekkah) in 570 CE and at the age of 40 received his first revelation from God through the angel Gabriel. As a result of these revelations from God, Muhammad became the founder of the Islamic faith and considered himself to be a prophet and messenger of God.

The term "Islam" is linguistically rooted in the word "peace," and shares much of its origins with earlier faiths of Judaism and Christianity. The Islamic holy book, the Qur'an (Koran), originated by Muhammad, includes many of the stories of the Old Testament including the same living God and similar prophets such as Adam, Noah, Moses, Elijah, John the Baptist, Jesus, and Muhammad. Among the early distinctions, however, is a more detailed account of the life of Jesus Christ than found in the New Testament, and in this account, Christ is viewed as a major prophet, not the son of God. Also, like the prophet Muhammad, it is the recorded belief of the Qur'an that Jesus was not crucified but ascended to Heaven by the hand of God. The Muslim belief is that Muhammad did not literally die and that he ascended to heaven alive

Muhammad has consistently been described as a mortal man, not divine, who experienced visions around the age of forty years in the form of direct communications with the angel, Gabriel, that expressed God's will. The holy text that resulted in the sixth century after Christ is given the Arabic title for "recitation." Rather than a narrative with a beginning, a middle, and end, the Qur'an is intended to be a statement of God's will in the form of Arabic poetry, advice, warnings, shared wisdom, and guidelines for maintaining the Islamic faith. The essence of that religion is also found in tenets known as The Five Pillars of Islamic Faith, and summarized very briefly as:

> *Shahadah* Profession of faith in the Oneness of God and accepting Muhammad as a messenger and prophet of God.
> *Salat* Requirement to pray five times each day at fixed times
> *Zakat* Concern for and giving of alms to the poor and unfortunate.
> *Sawm* Self-purification through fasting (especially during the month of Ramadan)
> *Hajj* Pilgrimage to Mecca at least once in a lifetime for those who are able.

Like Christianity and Judaism, Islam is represented by various points of view, but lacks the diversity of the two former religious groupings. In essence, there is the Sunni majority and the Shi'a minority with some variation of sects throughout the world. Islam is a religion that once spread from the western nations of Morocco and Spain to the eastern nations of India and China. In the distant past, Islam was a major rival to Christianity in the form of either voluntary or forced conversions. Islam continues to occupy much of the same geographic territory and continues to grow. It is the dominant religion of Indonesia, and approximately 85% or roughly 200 million residents of that island nation identify themselves as Muslims.

Islam is far more site-oriented than the other two great religions in focusing on "The Kaaba," a large cubical shrine faced with black stone in Mecca that all Muslims face during prayer. It is the destination site of the holy pilgrimage known as the Hajj, which is something that each capable Muslim must do at least once during his or her lifetime as an expression of faith.

Like Jesus Christ, Muhammad is said to have been born under an unusually bright star. Oddly, little is known about the youth, upbringing, or education of these two specific individuals who appear to be so visibly predestined to impact their world. Both men were of relatively humble origins, were publicly noticed at about age thirty and forty years respectively, and appear to have very powerful personal charismas based upon a new world view, not on wealth or acquired political power. Both men experienced visions that provided insights as to the mission of the remainder of their lives, and both men inspired many of their contemporaries and then dramatically ascended to Heaven. It is the legacy of these three great faiths, descended from Abraham of the Mesopotamian city of Ur, which has inspired and guided billions of people in positive and meaningful ways. The wicked twist of irony, however, is that the commonalities of these three great faiths are too often de-emphasized, and the resentments, distrust, and even senseless killing of persons of a different faith persisted for more than a millennia. The most fanatical and radical edge of each faith seems to cloak itself in a divinely inspired mission to take vengeance upon others who are not exactly like themselves. Like the capricious god or goddess of the ancient past whose behavior could only be described as vindictive and without motive, the fanatic fringe of the three great faiths that originated in the region of the Eastern Mediterranean seeks to impose its will and gain power by whatever means possible. The message of the great prophets is for them grossly distorted.

The acceptance and expansion of Islam, the most rapidly spreading faith of the three, is a matter of historic record and was a beacon of light after the Roman Empire had finally collapsed by 480 CE and much of Western Europe floundered in a period known as the Dark Ages. It was the Islamic faithful who made great efforts to acquire, translate, and preserve much of Europe's accumulated knowledge in the arts, sciences, and all other academic fields. Despite some setbacks as a result of the blood-drenched Crusades, there was an extended period of enlightenment within the Middle East that eventually expanded as far west as the great

Moorish universities at Toledo and Andalusia in Spain. However, following the final expulsion of the (Islamic) Moors from Spain in 1492, the European Renaissance, and early stages of the Industrial Revolution, the Islamic world appears to have drifted into a period of dormancy and even colonial subjugation by the "western powers." It has been mostly since World War II that Islam has reasserted its religious expansion and sought parity with the West along with avoidance of intrusions or dominance by the West.

Islamic geometrics

19
Creation Myths

"Every society is held together by a myth-system, a complex of dominating thought-forms that determines and sustains all its activities."

"All social relations, the very texture of human society, are myth-born and myth-sustained...."
    R.M. MacIver, *The Web of Government*
    (New York, The Macmillan Co., 1947), 4-5

"A culture isn't a rational invention-there are thousands of other cultures and they all work pretty well. All cultures function on faith rather than truth. There are lots of alternatives to our own society."
    Kurt Vonnegut, Playboy Interview, (Chicago,
    Playboy Magazine, July, 1973).

American Woodland Indian myth of twins born to a virgin mother who fell from the sky

"The woman from the sky originally comes from a hunting-culture base, and the woman of the earth comes from the planting culture. The twins represent two contrary principles, but quite different contrary principles from those represented by Cain and Abel in the Bible. In the Iroquois story, one twin is Sprout or Plant Boy, and the other is named Flint. Flint so damages his mother when he is born that she dies. Now, Flint and Plant Boy represent the two traditions. Flint is used for the blade to kill animals, so the twin named Flint represents the hunting tradition, and Plant Boy, of course, represents the planting principle.

In the biblical tradition, the plant boy is Cain and the flint boy is Abel, who is really a herder rather than a hunter. So in the Bible, you have the herder against the planter, and the planter is the one who is abominated. This is the myth of hunting people or herding people who have come into a planting-culture world and denigrate the people whom they have conquered."

      Joseph Campbell, *The Power of Myth* with
      Bill Moyers, (New York, Doubleday, 1988), 105.

Alternate Versions of the Woman Who Fell from the Sky

"Among the Iroquois, human life began when Skywoman was pushed out of her domain. She fell to an island that grew when a muskrat brought mud from under the sea and placed it in a turtle's shell. Turtle and island grew to make a home for Skywoman, who shortly gave birth to a daughter the beginning of the world."

      David Hurst Thomas, et al., *The Native Americans*
      An Illustrated History, (Atlanta, Turner Publishing,
      Inc., 1993) 37.

"Creation Legend [painting] by Tom Two-Arrows. The Iroquois creation story tells how white water birds met Skywoman as she descended onto a water-turtle the Earth. The Iroquois say that when the Earth cracks, the turtle is stretching."

      Onondaga tribe, *The Native Americans An*
      Illustrated History, (Atlanta, Turner Publishing,
      Inc., 1993), 106-07.

Coyote, the "Trickster"

"Coyote, the 'trickster,' appeared in a number of the oral traditions. He created things, caused trouble, got involved in many sexual escapades, and somehow always escaped the fate that would have overtaken a mere man. Coyote seemed human at times but was very clever. He and other supernatural heroes populated the literature and imaginations of Oregon's coastal peoples."

> *The First Oregonians*, (Portland, OR, Oregon Council for the Humanities, 1991), 7.

Creation Story of the Comanche

"One day the Great Spirit collected swirls of dust from the four directions in order to create the Comanche people. These people formed from the earth had the strength of mighty storms. Unfortunately, a shape-shifting demon was also created and began to torment the people. The Great Spirit cast the demon into a bottomless pit. To seek revenge the demon took refuge in the fangs and stingers of poisonous creatures and continues to harm people every chance it gets."

> Source David Hurst Thomas, *The Native Americans An Illustrated History*, (Atlanta, Turner Publishing, Inc., 1993), 108.

A Navajo Story

"A Navajo hogan, built in keeping with its creation myth "the Blessingway" when Talking God made the first hogan. The entrance faced east, to honor the sun, and bits of shell, obsidian, and turquoise would be set in the earth at the base of the support poles. Inside, men lived on the left, or south side, while the women lived on the north side. Everyone moved clockwise around the central hearth, in imitation of the movement of the sun. The hogan "like all things Navajo" was a mode of worship."

> David Hurst Thomas, *The Native Americans An Illustrated History*, (Atlanta, Turner Publishing, Inc., 1993), 310.

A Northwest Coast Story

"Raven was so lonely. One day he paced back and forth on the sandy beach feeling quite forlorn. Except for the trees, the moon, the sun, water and a few animals, the world was empty. His heart wished for the company of other creatures. Suddenly a large clam pushed through the sand making an eerie bubbling sound. Raven watched and listened intently as the clam slowly opened up. He was surprised and happy to see tiny people emerging from the shell. All were talking, smiling, and shaking the sand off their tiny bodies. Men, women, and children, spread around the island. Raven was pleased and proud with his work. He sang a beautiful song of great joy and greeting. He had brought the first people to the world."

> David Hurst Thomas, *The Native American An Illustrated History*, (Atlanta, Turner Publishing, Inc., 1993), 30.

Haida Mask

The Popol Vuh
An extract from *The Sacred Book of the Mayas*
University of Oklahoma Press, 1950

"This is the account of how all was in suspense, all calm, in silence; all motionless, still, and the expanse of the sky was empty. This is the first account, the first narrative. There was neither man, nor animal, birds, fishes, crabs, trees, stones, caves, ravines, grasses, nor forests there was only the sky. The surface of the earth had not appeared. There was only the calm sea and the great expanse of the sky. There was nothing brought together, nothing which could make a noise, nor anything which might move, or tremble or could make noise in the sky. There was nothing standing; only the calm water, the placid sea, alone and tranquil. Nothing existed. There was only immobility and silence in the darkness, in the night. Only the Creator, the Maker, Tepeu, Gucumatz, the Forefathers, were in the water surrounded with light. They were hidden under green and blue feathers, and were therefore called Gucumatz. By nature they were great sages and great thinkers...." Also see Stuart and Stuart, *The Mysterious Maya*, Washington, D.C., National Geographic Society, 1977).

Chichen Itza

Mesopotamian Myths

"The character of this religious system [Sumerian city-state theocracy] becomes more apparent once there are written copies of Mesopotamian myths and artistic representations of the gods and heroes. To the inhabitants of Mesopotamia the gods were many, for they represented the forces which drove mankind; and in primitive thought these forces were many, distinct in origin. Yet the gods were grouped in a regular pantheon.

Highest was An, the divine force, which could be visualized in the over-arching bowl of Heaven; his name meant 'sky' or 'shining.' Then came Enlil, the active force of nature, who at times, manifested himself in the raging storms of the plains, and at other times aided men. The goddess of the earth was worshipped as Nin-khursag, and under other names. Last of the four creator gods came Enki, the god of waters who fertilized the ground, and by extension became the patron of the skills of wisdom. To these were added 50 'great gods' who met in the assembly of the gods, the Annunaki; a host of other deities, demons, and the like also floated in the Mesopotamian spiritual world.

To the Sumerians their physical environment had come into being from a primordial chaos of water, whence the forces Tiamat and Abzu arose and, by processes of procreation, created the gods. Thereafter came the sky, the earth, and finally mankind...."

Chester A. Starr, *History of the Ancient World*,
(New York, Oxford University Press, 1965), 38.

Sumer and Akkad

"In the same way they told how the gigantic hero Gilgamesh, after many mighty deeds and strange adventures, failed to gain immortal life. Among these heroes, indeed, there was but one who was granted endless life. Of him there was a strange tale, telling how, together with his wife, he survived the great deluge [cf. Noah] in a large ship. Then the gods carried them both away to blessedness. But not even the kings of Sumer and Akkad were supposed to enter a blessed hereafter, much less the common people. Some of these stories of creation and flood were afterwards known to the Hebrews.

Mingled with touches from the life of both Sumerian and Semite, these tales now circulated in both the Semitic and Sumerian languages. It was the old Sumerian tongue, however, which was regarded as the more sacred. It was later continued in use as a kind of sacred language, like Latin in the Roman Catholic Church. The old Sumerian towns were now rapidly declining (twenty-third century B.C.), but religious stories were written in Sumerian, centuries after it was no longer spoken.

The period of the 'Kings of Sumer and Akkad' may be summarized as a century of splendor under the leadership of Ur (beginning about 2418 B.C.) and nearly three centuries of conflict and decline under her rivals, with Semitic kings in control. It was the classic age in the development of human life on the ancient Plain of Shinar, during which its essentially commercial character was stamped upon it. The fundamentals of its culture then assumed the form which they afterward retained, and things like law, business forms and custom, language and literature, and many other elements of culture gained their current and accepted character in the Age of Sumer and Akkad."

>James Henry Breasted, *The Conquest of Civilization*, (New York, Harper & Brothers Publishers, 1926), 143-44.

From Egalitarianism to Kleptocracy

"The remaining way for kleptocrats [i.e., priests] to gain public support is to construct an ideology or religion justifying kleptocracy. Bands and tribes already had supernatural beliefs, just as do modern established religions. But the supernatural beliefs of bands and tribes did not serve to justify central authority, justify transfer of wealth, or maintain peace between unrelated individuals. When supernatural beliefs gained those functions and became institutionalized, they were thereby transformed into what we term a religion. Hawaiian chiefs were typical of chiefs elsewhere, in asserting divinity, divine descent, or at least a hotline to the gods. The chief claimed to serve the people by interceding for them with the gods and reciting the ritual formulas required to obtain rain, good harvests, and success in fishing. Chiefdoms characteristically have an ideology, precursor to an institutionalized religion, that buttresses the chief's authority. The chief may either combine the offices of political leader and priest in a single person, or may support a separate group of kleptocrats (that is, priests) whose function is to provide ideological justification for the chiefs. That is why chiefdoms devote so much collected tribute to constructing temples and other public works, which serve as centers of the official religion and visible signs of the chief's power.

Besides justifying the transfer of wealth to kleptocrats, institutionalized religion brings two other important benefits to centralized societies. First, shared ideology or religion helps solve the problem of how unrelated individuals are to live together without killing each other by providing them with a bond not based on kinship. Second, it gives people a motive, other than genetic self-interest, for sacrificing their lives on behalf of others. At the cost of a few society members who die in battle as soldiers, the whole society becomes much more effective at conquering other societies or resisting attacks."

> Jared Diamond, *Guns, Germs, and Steel The Fates of Human Societies*, (New York, W. W. Norton & Company, 1999), 277-78.

Willamette Valley Myths

"Beyond the coastal mountains explored by Suku was the great valley of the Willamette River. The Kalapuya Indians lived throughout the valley. Below the falls of the Willamette resided the Clackamas and Clowewalla bands of Upper Chinook Indians. In Clackamas literature were many figures who belong to a Myth Age. They lived in a time before there were any humans. These myth figures included Panther Man, Bear Woman, Blue Jay Man, Skunk Man, and Coyote. In many ways these beings were humans and they often acted like humans. Yet, they also possessed an animal way to their acting. Blue Jay was often a troublemaker. Skunk Man was a fool and very unpleasant. Coyote, who appeared in many Indian tales in western Oregon, was sometimes daring. Other times Coyote helped everyone. Coyote might cause trouble or he might make things better again."

> Stephen Dow Beckham, *The Indians of Western Oregon* (Coos Bay, Arago Books, 1977), 10.

Adam and Eve (Adam and Lilith)

For comic effect and perhaps something more, Bill Maher's docudrama, Religulous, makes light of the credibility of a naked man and woman living alone in the woods and being influenced by a talking snake. It was an ideal set-up for a mythological tale that would include object lessons, a morality tale, or just good entertainment on cold winter nights, but not to be taken absolutely literally. For one thing, a less anthropomorphic interpretation of this creation story with only a few people to tell the tale might lead to the conclusion that snakes do not talk and that Adam used concealment or something like ventriloquism to project a voice other than his own and to convince Eve to do the one and only thing that had been proscribed by the deity.

The consequences for violating God's one and only rule included shame, eviction from a land of milk and honey in paradise, plus pain and suffering for all of humanity including their own immediate descendants. But, like virtually all morality tales, the forbidden deed is done and the consequences are harshly and permanently imposed on all of humanity as an object lesson.

The plot thickens rapidly even with such a small cast of characters. The only other possible culprits included a talking serpent; a God disguised as a serpent to test the one and only rule he had proscribed; a demon, not yet introduced to the story, who is in an on-going conflict with God and wants to prove that God's creation is morally weak and flawed; or Adam being a trickster with mixed motives to see how far he can push the only rule that he must obey. Although not specifically labeled "original sin" in the Bible, the single prohibition is violated, and weighs heavily on Eve (Lilith by some accounts) and the world's descendents.

The first man and first woman are traceable to virtually every culture that has taken the time to ponder such questions. The Adam and Eve story has its roots in early Babylonian mythology as a nursery tale invented by female royals within the early monarchies and has been perpetuated and likely altered over many thousands of years in that part of the eastern Mediterranean. The story makes sense to children between the ages of three and six years. A more sophisticated story would simply involve the creation of a group of unrelated men and women who started out the first colony. The problem with only one man and one woman is that the third generation of humans has no alternative but to be based on the mating of brothers and sisters. Such biological incest has generally been viewed as a sin by most cultures. Also, the story about the hunter, Cain, slaying the farmer, Abel, may be viewed as a morality tale to stress the consequences of sibling rivalry leading to homicide. Mythology is often intended to frame one or more object lessons about life in colorful and memorable ways. To have faith in what we are told as children by adults, it is also critical to have logical actions and consequences where possible without relying on magic, or mysterious and unfathomable behavior of the gods.

Native American Tales

"Other Indian tales of creation portray the sky as a great source of power and enlightenment, but one that must first be wedded to the earth in order to bring benefits. Zuni legend asserts that at the dawn of time, Mother Earth and Father Sky lay together in the primordial waters in a fertile embrace. Growing large with her offspring, Mother Earth then separated herself from Father Sky and slid beneath the waters. In a similar story told by the Luiseno people of coastal California, life began with formless energies that were male and female [that] drifted close to each other in the endless void. The female spoke first saying, 'I am that which stretches out flat.' The male replied, 'I am that which arches over everything.' After this brief introduction, they made love and produced the 'thoughts' of all that was to come.
According to the oral tradition of the Okanagon a people inhabiting the sagebrush flats of a Columbia River tributary, a mysterious creator, known as the chief of spirits, formed the earth out of a woman. 'You will be the mother of all people,' the chief told the earth, and as such, her spirit lives on. As the tales re-

lates, 'the soil is her flesh, the rocks are her bones, the wind her breath, trees and grass her hair. She lives spread out, and we live on her. Whenever she moves, we have an earthquake.'

Within the lands of every tribe are certain sacred placesmountains, lakes, woodlands, or canyons- that are believed to harbor extraordinary power. These revered landmarks figure prominently in the legends of many Indian peoples. The creation stories of the Navajo, for example, describe the formation of the four distinctive peaks or mountain chains that border their ancestral homeland at each quarter in the present-day Four Corners region, where the states of Utah, Colorado, Arizona, and New Mexico converge. According to one Navajo legend, First Man and First Woman created those sacred mountains from soil that First Man had stored along with other magical substances in his medicine bundle. The couple then fastened down Blanca Peak in the east with a bolt of white lightning and covered it with a blanket of daylight. They pinned Mount Taylor in the south with a stone knife and draped it in blue. They fastened the San Francisco Peaks in the west with a sunbeam and cloaked them with yellow. And they tied down Hesperus Peak in the north with a rainbow and shrouded it in darkness. From that time forward, the Navajo associated each direction with a special color and power white for the lightning to the east, blue for the sky to the south yellow for the sun to the west, and black for storm clouds to the north." *The Spirit World*, (Alexandria, VA, Time-Life Books,1992), 27, 30.

An American Tragedy of Timing and Circumstance

One of the tragic moments in human history was the discovery of the Americas by European adventurers at the peak of the

Spanish Inquisition. The threat of the continued Islamic presence of the Moors in Spain had just ended when Columbus was funded by Ferdinand and Isabella, Spanish monarchs, to outfit three small ships for an unprecedented voyage of discovery. Once discovered, however, the Native Americans were routinely given the choice of immediate religious conversion, exploitation of their labor, or death. The deadliest introduction from Europe, however, was in the form of deadly microbes for which the Native Americans had little or no resistance. Half a millennium later the consequences of that untimely discovery are still felt. As an additional result, virtually all of the rich mythologies and histories of millions of diverse people living in the Americas for thousands of years were lost or almost completely lost.

West Coast Native American wood carved mask

20
The Afterlife of Myth and Religion

Life's final journey is common to all things. Without exception, all life is finite. What comes after for all living things is the question that humanity has sought to answer for all of its known existence. Each culture, each religion, and each period of time has reflected on both the tragedy and the potential glory of life's final passages. The response has been varied.

The ancient Greek perception of the afterlife has much in common with contemporary religious beliefs. In ancient times, the recently deceased were thought to be escorted on a journey to the underworld by benevolent gods. Typically, that passage involved the payment of a modest fee by one or more survivors that would go with the earthly body as payment to a mythological ferryman. That god's name was Charon and it was his responsibility to transport the spirit of the newly deceased to the other side of the River Styx. Once there, the spirit was judged and allowed to either enter paradise or condemned to an eternity of suffering in a hellish environment. Provision was made for borderline individuals who served a period of penitence and were allowed to enter paradise at a later time.

Egyptians were among the first of the civilized nations to focus much of their political and religious beliefs on the prospect of attaining an immortal afterlife. In a top-down culture where royalty was synonymous or almost synonymous with divinity, attaining a rich and comfortable afterlife was a conscious goal of the elite from the time of their birth. Burial chambers evolved from simple bench-like structures to massive block pyramids and tombs that were carved into solid limestone. The burial site contained the recognizable physical body of the deceased, their name, and items considered essential for their next life in paradise. The elaborate and challenging passage into the afterlife evolved in complexity as life itself became increasingly complex, ritualized, and intimately involved with a vast assortment of god and goddesses who would share eternity with those who were admitted to paradise. Increasingly, those who could afford an elaborate burial sought admittance to an afterlife of ease in a setting comparable to their life in Egypt.

Sumerians exhibited a lust for living in comparison to the conservative Hebrews who concentrated on traditions and compliance with fairly repressive laws intended to please their God. The early Sumerians described the transition from the realm of the living to the realm of the dead in their literature as a journey to the underworld. That journey was escorted by the goddess, Inanna. It was the spirit, not the body that transcended into the netherworld where emotional and physical desires were often frustrated. It was only through the intervention of the gods that the deceased were able to fulfill needs and desires in the absence of a physical body. Little detail appeared to be given to actual conditions in the afterlife and, especially for the non-elite, immortality was a dreary prospect in a featureless environment under the control of the gods.

Biblical references to life after death are typically not mentioned in great detail. There were about 24 different Jewish groups in the first century BCE who held a wide range of beliefs about life after death. The Sadducees, for instance, described death as a cessation of life. The Pharisees, of which St. Paul was a proponent, described a conditional admission to heaven. It was

Jesus Christ, John the Baptist, and the Essenes who instilled a concept of resurrection after death and emphasized the potential that even "the least among us" could share in the potential for admission to an afterlife in heaven. Later interpretations are generally very specific to each faith group and tend to place major restrictions on admission to heaven and place much focus on the prospects for damnation in hell.

Hebrew beliefs in the earliest times had much in common with their Mesopotamian neighbors. Death tended to be viewed essentially as an end of life where the soul or essence of the person's spirit would dwell within a heaven established by a benevolent God, not humanities' wishful fantasies of how it would be. The image of heaven contained a small degree of differentiation based on how each person had led their life. But for devout Hebrews there was far less emphasis on punishment or judgment of the just and unjust after death. The major focus of Judaism has been on the present life, not the glories of a life to be experienced after death. One practical admonition to be found in early writings is that the righteous will be reunited with family and loved ones after death and the non-righteous will not. The Torah, for example, suggests an obsession with the present world and encourages avoidance of prolonged contact with dead bodies. Faith in the afterlife instead relies on the benevolence of God and of deference to God's plan whatever that may be. Unlike the ancient Egyptians who invested endless time and attention to details about the afterlife, the more rational approach of the Hebrews focuses on present realities, not the unknowable afterlife that cannot be verified.

Persian mythology details the journey into the afterlife. Each deceased person was required to cross a bridge called the Chinvat Passage. The bridge was wide and allowed easy crossing for those deserving souls who could then continue on to heaven. Passage was arduous and the bridge was as thin as the sharp edge of a knife blade for those who had been wicked. They would usually fail to get across and instead tumbled into a hellish environment for eternity. A later refinement by the Zoroastrian religion beginning about 1000 BCE included a final judgment where the world would be consumed in a global fire which would cleanse the world of evil. The wicked and evil souls would suffer the most from the flames but once purified they could join their brethren in an afterworld free of evil.

In the Norse afterlife, Valhalla was reserved for warriors who died in combat. One requirement was that approximately one half of that group (einherjar) would maintain their readiness to fight in the epic final battle known as Ragarok. More commonly, Norse clans anticipated a dreary subterranean otherworld where they would continue their existence in ways similar to their lives among the living. The main distinction was that life after death was more clearly governed by select gods and goddesses.

The afterlife plays a critical role in Islamic beliefs. Islam shares much about the afterlife with their Judaic and Christian predecessors. There is a clear visualization of a paradise for those judged to be good and a hell for those judged to be persistently bad or evil. The moment of judgment is thought to be based on answers that the recently departed give to designated angels. It is the responsibility of the angels to make a final determination. Ultimately, there is the potential for a resurrection based on a final judgment from God. In the interim prior to judgment, the physical life of the body ends and the spirit rests. Finally, once judgment arrives each person will be judged on actual deeds during their life and the pure will ascend to heaven.

For the ancient Aztecs who lived without known contact with people outside of the western hemisphere in the pre-Columbian Period, the afterlife was a cyclical event. Death was viewed as a continuation of the original life force that united all of humanity. Birth was considered a release from the spirit world and death was the return to that world. The souls of the deceased inhabited the invisible spirit world with the gods. In following sacred rituals the Aztec rulers and shamans were able to communicate with that otherworld and in that way preserved the cycle of life and death.

Many early pagan beliefs tended to acknowledge death as an extension of life. That afterlife could be fulfilled in an altered yet continued existence in a spiritual paradise, reincarnation, or a cessation of all existence for a specific person. The impact and potential for increased interaction with assorted gods and goddesses in a new realm was therefore inevitable. It was due to the potential for conflicts among the competing personalities of the gods that life after death for mortals remained ill-defined. Thus, the incentive to lead a positive life with the best interests of others in mind was its own reward, not a directive or threat of punishment from the gods. The concept of reincarnation possibly evolved from the desire to carry forward the positive thoughts, feelings, and deeds of ancestors. For highly regarded family and friends there was the potential that the recently deceased person could pass along something positive about their existence to the lives of those living in the present.

21
Egyptian Gods and Goddesses

Egypt set the standard for western religions on a very grand scale. Within a period of at least 3,000 years and beginning with prehistory, a richly complex orchestra of gods and goddesses evolved out of early mankind's need for answers to major questions and events within their day-to-day lives. With the rising sun each day there was the appearance of birth of a god-like force that was absolutely essential to the lives and well-being of the inhabitants of that confined region bordering on the world's largest river. We know with much certainty that our earliest prehistory ancestors showed great reverence for that divine-like force that sustained their daily lives, their crops, and the broader world around them. On the dark side, there was also the setting sun each day that returned the world to a potential for chaos, non-growth, and even death. Our living, breathing ancestors of the prehistory world were intimately aware of the finality and irreversible tragedy of death. The alternative to the paralyzing fear of death, to fear that the sun may not return the next day, is to attribute divine forces to identifiable superhuman beings with the power to raise the sun each day, to prevent utter chaos, and to provide meaning for the unknowns and complexities of daily existence. In that prehistoric world, the mythological explanation within the small group that best accounts for difficult-to-understand events begins to take on an artificial life, evolves, and provides answers for what was otherwise unknowable. Eventually the power of repetition, familiarity, and enriched embellishments of what came to be (superhuman) gods and goddesses became an inseparable part of ancient Egyptian reality. Local gods and regional gods tended to proliferate, evolve, sometimes morph into anthropomorphic gods, and diversify as needs arose until there were literally well over 1,000 gods and goddesses whose relevance and powers would vary from place to place and time to time. It was the scale of ancient Egypt's religion that was so profound. The multi-room bench-like tomb for a deceased pharaoh (mastabas) evolved into the grand pyramids that remain today. Small worship sites evolved into temples that remain among the largest and most distinctive in world history.

It was the early focus on the afterlife and preservation or extension of life in the paradise-like conditions of the Nile River Valley that also set ancient Egypt's polytheistic religion apart. Early on, the association with death and preservation of the human body in a life-like condition facilitated that person's essence to move forward and dwell forever in an idealized afterlife. In life after death, which was reluctantly extended beyond the highest ranks of the royals and the priesthood, there was the increased potential to communicate with gods and to curry favor for those who remained alive and their future generations. As the pharaoh assumed more and more of the trappings of being a living link to various gods and of assuming elements of divinity, it was believed that direct communication with the gods was improved. This connectedness with specific gods increased the authority and power of the monarchy, the priesthood, and helped to justify grand and grander construction projects. Such massive structures created a sense of shock and awe among the populace and groups living outside of Egypt that might be a threat to the populace or the theocracy at the top. A classic example of the principle can be found today near Egypt's southern border. One of the world's great treasures was commissioned during the reign of Rameses II and named Abu Simbel for the local shepherd boy who re-discovered the almost entirely sand-covered site in 1813. The discovery was conveyed to Swiss explorer, Johann

Burckhardt, and he was guided to the site by the young boy. After major excavation, the Great Temple of Rameses II and the smaller Temple of Queen Nefertari were again revealed in their full glory. The seated statues of Rameses II , Amun, Ra-Horakhty, and Ptah are 67 feet high in a seated position. The two temples were intended to place Rameses II on a par with Egypt's most important gods and to intimidate the Nubian people to the south who had been historic rivals as well as trading partners.

One of the oldest anthropomorphic gods of the ancient Egyptian religion is remembered best by the Greek name of Anubis. Sculptures and inscriptions of this central figure in their pantheon of gods are usually represented as a man with the exaggerated head of a jackal. In the earliest of times it was noted that packs of jackals (similar to an African wild dog) were observed at burial sites and, as scavengers, were prone to dig at those sites to consume the flesh of the dead. The association with the dead was made during pre-recorded times and was soon paired with assumptions about the afterlife and the ritualized process for attaining a proper afterlife, i.e., mummification. As a god, Anubis was occasionally illustrated as a stylized full jackal but more often as a man with a jackal's head who took responsibility as a protector of the dead and the eternal resting places of the dead. In that process of remembering and honoring their dead, the ancient Egyptian culture focused on the concept of the afterlife to the point of obsession. The earliest thrust of that cultural obsession likely focused on their king and the royal family to ensure that good communication with other gods was favorably maintained in the best interests of the populace. Perhaps simultaneously, the burgeoning monarchies and priesthood would recognize the loosely defined promise of the afterlife as a potent mechanism to influence positive and negative behaviors of the masses. The concept of immortality in a positive setting for their deceased royals and highest level priests would bode well for everyone. The Egyptian Book of the Dead actually shows the god, Anubis, performing the weighing of the heart ceremony that represented "objective" proof that the deceased subject led a good life. The judgment was in the form of a scale of justice and truth. The ceremony was witnessed by other all-knowing gods who judged one's lifetime of behavior to establish that person's rightful place in the afterlife. The heart, to the ancient Egyptians, was considered the center of memory, thought, and emotion. If there was sufficient wrong-doing, the heart was grabbed from the scale and devoured by a fearsome beast with the enormous head of a crocodile, the front legs of a lion, and the body and hind legs of a hippopotamus (Ammit, the non-divine "gobbler"). Variations of Anubis continued throughout ancient Egyptian history until the Second or Third century CE when images of the part-animal and part-human god were mocked by the Greeks and the Romans as the "barker god." During Egypt's Middle Kingdom, Anubis was displaced by Osiris as the protector of the dead. According to an ancient myth it was Anubis who assisted the god, Isis, in bringing her husband, Osiris, back to life. Ironically, with changing myths over time, there are conflicts about the origins of Anubis. By another account, Anubis was the son of Osiris by Nephthys (sister of Isis) in an adulterous affair that led one god to kill another. The husband of Nephthys, Seth, the god of chaos, killed his brother-in-law, Osiris, by first using molten lead to seal him in a coffin and then to sail it down the Nile. Isis learned of the incident and searched until she located the coffin on the banks of the Eastern Mediterranean near present-day Lebanon. She restored him to life (his first resurrection) and within one tradition they conceived the god, Horus. By other accounts, the parents of the ancient god, Horus, were Osiris and Hathor. However, once Seth learned of this, he killed Osiris a second time and dismembered the body to make a possible search by Isis even more difficult. All of Osiris' body parts except for the phallus were eventually found and the god of all living things, human, animal, and vegetation, was again resurrected. Then, Osiris, son of Geb, god of the earth, and Nut, goddess of the sky, assumed responsibility to judge the souls of the dead with a focus on immortality. As an early example of resurrection of the dead, he was venerated as the god of regeneration and re-birth of all things. He was forever known as the god of the underworld and of the afterlife. He was even associated with the flooding and retreating of the life-giving Nile. Osiris was thus one of the best known and most popular of the ancient Egyptian gods.

The sustaining force of the sun god from the earliest times in Egyptian history evolved over several thousand years but did not seriously fade until the final breakdown of the monarchy around the time of the introduction of Christianity and the fall of the Roman Empire. Ultimately, Amun (Amun-Ra) was worshipped as the king of Egyptian gods, the creator deity and the sun-god who was also responsible for the wind and many different aspects of Egyptian life. He was the regional patron deity of the capital city of Thebes and as his popularity grew, he acquired or possessed many overlapping powers with the all-powerful early gods, Ptah and Osiris. In that process associations were made with the sun-god, Ra-Herakhty, of other regions and the result was a merging of the powers and identities of the sun-god, Ra, and of Horus, the protector god.

The single exception during the two-thousand-year history of Egyptian gods and goddesses actually followed the growing popularity of Amun-Ra. For a very brief period of perhaps a dozen years in the history of the ancient world's longest surviving and perhaps oldest large-scale civilization, one eccentric pharaoh proclaimed a ban on all former Egyptian gods and insisted upon the worship of a single, all-powerful sun-god, the Aten. The unsuccessful experiment with monotheism was ruthlessly crushed in a manner that appears to be lost to the historic record and the former gods, including Amun-Ra, were restored and were in place for more than an additional one thousand years.

Ancient Egyptian Gods and Goddesses

Aker	Associated with underworld. Usually two back-to-back lions
Amaunet	(goddess) Represents hidden powers. Represented with a snake's head
Ammit	(goddess) Consumes heart at judgment. Humanoid with head of crocodile
Amun	King of gods. Humanoid with ram's head and double plume headdress
Anat	Goddess of war. A woman with axe, lance, and shield dressed for battle
Anubis	A jackal or jackal-headed male. Associated with embalming and burials
Anuket	(goddess) A woman with plumed headdress. Associated with hunting
Apis	Has the appearance of a bull and is associated with power and fertility
Apophis	Appears as a snake and represents chaos and an enemy to the sun god
Arensnuphis	Appears as a man with plumed crown. Associated with the Nubians
Astarte	(goddess) A naked woman on horseback with horns or crown. Associated with war
Aten Briefly	represented as sun disk with rays. Akhenaten's monotheistic supreme god

Atum	A man with a Nemes headdress. A creator god associated with the sun
Baal	A man with beard and helmet with horns (Syrian). Associated with sky & storms
Baba	A baboon god. Associated with aggression and the male penis
Banebdjedet	Appears as a ram. Associated with the sky and virility
Bastet	(goddess) Appears as a cat or with cat's head. Associated with maternalism
Bat	(goddess) Appears as a woman with cow's ears and horns. Associated with fertility, sky
Benu	Appears as a heron. Associated with daily rebirth of the sun
Bes	Appears as a dwarf lion. Associated with childbirth and household matters
Buchis	Appears as a bull and is a manifestation of Re/Ra or Osiris
Duamutef	A jackal-headed god. Associated with mummification (stomach + upper intestines)
Geb	Appears as man with Red Crown or goose on his head. Associated with earth's fertility
Hapu	Associated with healing. Humanoid appearance
Hapy	A man with breasts and headdress of aquatic plants or baboon. Associated with floods
Hathor	(goddess) A woman with cow's ears, horns, and often sun disk on head. Fertility, love
Hatmehyt	(goddess) Appears as a lepidotus fish.
Hauhet	(goddess) Appears as a snake-headed woman. An ancient god of floods
Heket	(goddess) Appears as a frog or with a frog's head. Associated with childbirth

Herishef ....Appears with ram's head and long horns and sun disk. Associated with solar forces
Horus ....A falcon-headed man, or a falcon. God of sky, a protector of king and people
Hu ....Appears as a man. A symbol of authority; divine utterance
Ihy ....Appears as a child or young man. A child of the gods Hathor and Horus
Imhotep ....Appears as a seated man holding papyrus roll Associated with wisdom and medicine
Imsety ....Appears as a man. Associated with canopic functions (liver), and the direction south
Ipy (Ipet)............(goddess) Appears as a hippopotamus. Associated with magic and protection
Ishtar ....(goddess) Appears as a woman. Associated with battle, sexuality, fertility and healing
Isis.....................(goddess) Appears in a royal headdress. Associated with magic, wife/sister of Osiris
Kauket................(goddess) Appears with head of snake. Associated with the primeval and with darkness
Khepri ....Appears as scarab beetle or man with such a head. Associated with creation and the sun
Khnum ....Appears as a ram or ram-headed man. Associated with creation, pottery, and fertile soil
Khonsu..............Appears as a child with moon headdress. Associated with different phases of the moon
Kuk ....Appears with a frog's head. Associated with darkness and primeval factors
Maat ....(goddess) Has a single feather and cobra headdress. Associated with justice, order, truth
Mafdet................(goddess) Appears as a woman or a panther. A protector against scorpions and snakes
Mandulis ....Has ram's horns, plumes, sun-disk, and cobras. Associated with sun and Upper Nile

Mehen ....Appears as a coiled snake. Associated with protection of the sun god
Mehet-Weret ......(goddess) Appears as a cow. Associated with sky and potential for flooding
Mertseger ....(goddess) Appears as a cobra. A protector of silence
Meskhenet..........(goddess) A mud brick with a human head. Goddess of childbirth; destiny
Min.....................Appears as a man with erection. Associated with fertility, harvest, and mining
Mnevis ....Appears as a bull. Associated with the sun god; oracles
Montu.................A falcon or a man with falcon-head, sun disk, and plumes. Associated with war
Mut.....................(goddess) Appears as a vulture. Associated with motherhood
Naunet................(goddess) Appears as snake-headed woman. Associated with primordial waters
Nefertem ....A lion-headed man with a lotus headdress. Associated with powers of the lotus
Neith ....(goddess) A woman with red crown, shield, and crossed arrows. Warfare and weaving
Nekhbet..............(goddess) Appears as a vulture. A local goddess of Upper Egypt
Neper ....Appears as a man. Associated with the harvest of grain
Nephthys ....(goddess) Appears as a woman with a basket headdress. Protection and funerals
Nun ....A frog or baboon-headed man. Associated with primordial waters
Nut ....(goddess) Appears as a woman or as a cow. Associated with the sky; sarcophagus
Onuris ....A bearded man with four-plume headdress. Associated with warriors; hunters

Osiris .... A mummified man with crook and flail. God of afterlife, death, rebirth, and fertility
Pakhet .... (goddess) Appears as a lioness. A guardian of the gates
Ptah .... A partially mummified man with skull cap and scepter. A creator of gods, craftsmen
Qadesh .... (goddess) A nude woman standing on a lion. Associated with sexual pleasure
Qebehsenuef ...... Appears as a falcon-headed man. A canopic god (lower intestines).
Re or Ra .... A ram or falcon-headed man with sun disk and cobra. The primary sun god; creator
Renenutet .... (goddess) Appears as a cobra. Associated with nursing, harvests, and war
Reshef/Reshep ... A bearded man with white crown. Associated with war (Amorite)
Sah .... Appears as a man. Associated with the constellation of Orion
Satet .... (goddess) A woman in white crown with antelope horns. Protector of the southern border
Sekhmet .... (goddess) A lion or lion-headed with disk. Associated with healing and destruction
Selket .... (goddess) A woman with a scorpion headdress. Associated with funerals; protection
Seshat .... (goddess) A woman in panther-skin robe and seven-point star on her head.
Seth .... A man with animal head. Associated with chaos, infertility, storms, and evil
Shu .... A lion-headed man with feather on head. Associated with the air
Sia .... Appears as a man. Associated with divine knowledge, intellectual achievement

Sobek	A crocodile or croc-headed man. Associated with the pharaoh's powers to rule
Sokar	A mummified man with a crown of horns. Associated with funerary activities
Sopdet/Sothis	(goddess) A woman with a star on her head. Associated with "Dog Star"
Tatenen	A man with two-plume crown and ram's horns. Fertility of Nile silt, floods, vegetation
Taweret	(goddess) A hippo with parts from a lion and crocodile. Associated with childbirth
Tayet	(goddess) Appears as a woman. Associated with weaving
Tefnut	(goddess) Appears as a lioness-headed woman with cobra. "Eye of Re" (moisture)
Thoth	A baboon or ibis-headed man. Associated with moon, scribes, and knowledge
Wadjet/Edjo	(goddess) Appears as a lioness or cobra. Mascot goddess of Lower Egypt

Ancient God Horus Relief

22
The Hittites

The Hittite Empire of the eastern Mediterranean from roughly 1800 BCE to 1200 BCE rivaled and impacted the Egyptians, the Canaanites, the Assyrians, and the Babylonians. It was a time of warring city-states, population explosions, technological innovations, rampant paganism, and cultural/political obsession to be dominant or risk domination by others. The Hittite people were a composite of Indo-European, Indo-Iranian, and Indo-Aryan origin and inhabited much of the present nation of Turkey (Anatolia). They were drawn from a broad regional base that includes much of present-day western Russia, Syria, Iran (ancient Persia), Iraq (ancient Babylon), and Lebanon. These hardy people gave great credence to the cult of the pagan warrior, yet possessed an advanced legal system, and a rich mythology that influenced the Old Testament, the Greeks, and the Romans. The upper echelons were literate, had a disciplined sense of their history, language, culture, and left a legacy of at least 25,000 cuneiform clay tablets that have been mostly deciphered. To the ancient Egyptians they were the fierce, bearded barbarians to the north who were trade partners and a periodic threat to their existence. The Hittite language was heavily dependent upon dialects of Akkadian and Sumerian languages of Mesopotamia that had evolved from oral traditions and later from symbolic glyphs to more abstract cuneiform writing to meet the demands of growing city-states.

Around 1650 BCE the Hittite city-states consolidated their military power, advanced metallurgy, and superior chariot design to represent a very substantial threat to the region. Their king, Hattusili I, amassed wealth and power and assumed many of the attributes of a deity. It was only after several setbacks in his military campaigns that he withdrew from an ambitious plan to control much of the ancient world. Out of fear for their own survival, the Assyrians and the Egyptians formed a coalition to stop the Hittite onslaught into their territories. By 1595 BCE, the king's grandson, Mursili I, was able to refocus their conquests and defeated the Babylonians. Communities that submitted to Hittite rule were spared and those who resisted were exterminated with no sign of mercy. It was at this approximate time that the Israelite Exodus out of northeastern Egypt occurred and followed a circuitous route to avoid confrontation with Egyptian troops stationed in the region of present Gaza plus the Hittites and Babylonians to the north and east for a reported period of forty years. The Israelites then spent the next four centuries reassimilating into the land of Canaan without being devoured by the big power players of the Near East.

One of the cultural distinctions of the Hittite people was a tendency to adopt the pagan gods, goddesses, and mythologies or folklore of the people they dominated. Ultimately, there was a great amount of confusion as local and regional deities could be identified with virtually every aspect of human existence and literally numbered into the thousands. The concept of divinity was quite broadly applied as well. A king, for instance, might describe himself as an adopted child of a god. Without directly calling himself a god, he might say, "When my father became a god." From an early time there was the issue of legitimate, usually hereditary, right to become a king that set an individual and his family apart from the masses. It is just a short step from that preordained sense of exclusivity to feel a god-given right to be in some way divine as well. Ironically, it was often a circuitous path in claiming the legal right to the throne. One family member assassinating another was at times the norm rather than the exception. Such acts of violence had to be done in surreptitious ways to avoid plunging a kingdom into a period of chaos and civil war.

Another distinction of the Hittite people was a sophisticated legal system that was based on compensation for wrong-doing, not retribution such as was so typical of eastern Mediterranean cultures. The ancient model for revenge was an obligation that was often passed from one generation to another for extended periods of time. By the time of the Babylonian King Hammurabi, there was a distinct effort to improve the severe and excessive inequities of the old legal system. A more equitable form of justice placed limits on retribution in the form of "an eye for an eye and a tooth for a tooth." This new mandate was intended to limit the extreme forms of retribution that usually accompanied the overly subjective high crimes of sorcery, adultery, and murder. Perhaps the extremist form of retribution for crimes, especially crimes against the state, was in the form of crucifixion, which probably originated in the ancient Persian Empire prior to 400 BCE. The method, which was intended to produce pain, suffering, humiliation, and visual deterrence to the extreme, was also used against pirates in the port of Athens around the seventh century BCE. The heinous practice was re-introduced by Alexander the Great throughout his empire in the fourth century BCE. The practice eventually crept as far west as Carthage in northern Africa where the Romans used the execution method freely with errant slaves, criminals, and despised enemies of the empire. Near the time of Christ's birth one of the three Roman emperors of the Triumvirate, Crassus, put down the Spartacus slave rebellion that so severely humiliated ancient Rome by crucifying almost 6,000 slaves along the 125-mile road from Capua to Rome. The victims were typically humiliated in the extreme by being stripped naked and then fastened to a capital T-shaped cross that barely elevated the victim's feet off of the ground. The intent was to cause a horrific, slow, and painful death due to a combination of dehydration and asphyxiation that could take many days to accomplish. The bodies were then left to decompose or were otherwise treated with official contempt. The rebellious slaves led by Spartacus had ultimately been betrayed by pirates who reneged on a plan to transport them by ship from the southern tip of Italy to the island of Sicily. The mental image of such a grotesque execution of so many human beings and indifference by those in authority was certainly not lost on the Roman province of Palestine where crucifixion continued to be practiced around the time of Jesus Christ.

By 1525 BCE, the Hittites had lost most of their extensive territory after the assassination of King Mursili I by his brother-in-law, followed by a period when the kingdom was plunged into chaos, rampant disease, and petty wars. The once-great capital of Hattusha, a 400-acre walled city with clay-pipe plumbing, stone blocks weighing up to 40 tons, and most of the accoutrements of an advanced empire comparable to either Babylon or Thebes, was a shadow of its former size and glory. In time the Egyptians aligned with the people of Mitanni (current Iraq) to further neutralize the power of the Hittite people. The Pharaoh Amenhotep III, in fact, noted that the Hittite people were effectively paralyzed and thought to be destroyed. However, like the phoenix returning from the ashes, the greatest king of the Hittite people, Shuppiluliuma I, was instrumental in rebuilding the army and systematically re-establishing Hittite power and vast regional control through a combination of military victories and treaties signed under the threat of annihilation. The Mitanni kingdom was the last to fall. Also, like pharaohs of the past, Hittite King Shuppiluliuma dismissed his wife/queen to marry the daughter of a Babylonian king as a further extension of his rebuilt empire. This king was perhaps the most powerful monarch in the entire region of the Near East and Egypt when he was approached in writing by the young widow of King Tutankhamun, Ankhesenamun. It has long been rumored that in apparent desperation, the widowed queen (or a designated representative) sent a letter offering to marry one of the Hittite king's sons in a fleeting attempt to consolidate and retain her power as the queen of Upper and Lower Egypt, and to avoid a forced marriage to the elderly Chancellor/Vizier Aye. Shuppiluliuma, however, had concerns about a possible deception yet sent one of his sons to marry her. Then, after several weeks elapsed the wily old king learned that his son had been murdered by rival military forces of the disgraced queen as the entourage was about to cross the border into Egypt.

In a fearsome rage, Hittite King Shuppiluliuma brought all of his military might down on the Egyptians and proceeded to destroy one Egyptian town and settlement after another. In the process many captured Egyptians were forcibly taken northward as slaves. The irony of the crushing war due to royal intrigues was that many of the captive Egyptians were sick with a deadly plague that suddenly devastated the Hittite lands. Their entire empire was reduced to virtual starvation as the empire collapsed over a twenty-year period of plague like the Black Death that terrorized Europe in the Middle Ages. The surviving power structure of the Hittite people turned to an oracle for guidance and they ultimately blamed Shuppiluliuma for the devastation. The gods supposedly found fault with the old king for murdering his brother to acquire the throne and for attacking Egypt without the approval of the storm god.

Shuppiluliuma's son, Moshili, assumed power by 1279 BCE. He recognized that the greatest threat to the Hittite Empire was from Egypt to the south. Being an ambitious and able warrior himself, Moshili had brought the Plains of Kadesh under Hittite rule by 1274 BCE and had laid a trap to destroy the 20,000-man army of Rameses II. It was only by a last-minute miracle that Rameses II was not totally defeated after splitting his forces many times and accepting the lies of two intentionally captured Bedouin spies. Almost half of Rameses' army was captured or destroyed, but the Hittites failed to aggressively pursue their victory. The situation finally became an impasse and Rameses II declared a victory at Kadesh. Few were in a position to dispute his claims. Oddly enough, there have been biblical researchers who have claimed that the Exodus followed this turmoil between the Hittites and Egypt in the year 1267 BCE. This would be the latest date for speculation on the actual date for Moses to lead an entire colony of Israelite people out of the Delta region of Egypt. This date would be generations after the speculative suggestion that Akhenaten transcended into the biblical Moses. There was also speculation that a high priest at the end of Akhenaten's failed reign exploited the dissention of the moment and persuaded huge numbers of Israelites in Egypt to risk everything and seek a new homeland that they would have to take by force. It is for the reader to continue the challenge of accurately identifying the true time period for Moses' Exodus out of Egypt. Factual, documented data does not necessarily detract from the Old Testament's Book of Exodus, but in fact helps to confirm certain biblical/historical events in a more accurate context and allows the researcher to identify erroneous information that cannot possibly be true. Stories that are found to be fabricated myths can still be retained for their entertainment value and possible value as allegorical lessons about human behavior with or without pagan gods and goddesses.

Hittite Gods & Goddesses

Alalu .... An original king of heaven prior to removal by his son, Anu(s)
Anu(s) .... A sky god who was first among the gods until removed by his son, Kumarbis
Aranzahas ..... A deification of the Tigris River
Arinna .... The sun goddess
Astabis .... The god of warriors
Ea .... A possible father of the Storm god who assisted in the defeat of Ulikummis
Enlil .... Originally a leader of the pantheon of gods
Hannahannas. Queen of Heaven, mother of all gods, prone to fits of anger
Hasamelis...... A protection god for travelers
Hebat............. A sun goddess and wife of the storm god, Teshub(a)
Hedammu...... A serpent god
Illuyankas...... A legendary dragon god
Imbaluris .... A messenger god for Kumarbis
Inaras .... A daughter of the Storm god and goddess of wild animals
Ishtar .... A seductress god represented as a lioness
Isirra.............. Multiple goddesses who do the bidding of other gods
Kamrusepas .. A goddess of healing and magic
Kashku .... The moon god
Kubaba.......... A chief goddess
Kumarbis ...... The high god of the Hittites, The father of all gods who chased off Anu(s)
Mezzullas...... A daughter of the storm god and sun god who can influence her parents
Mukisanus..... Chief advisor to Kumarbis

Nerik .... A weather god
Seris .... A mythological bull sacred to the storm god
Shaushka .... The love goddess
Storm gods .... Variously chief gods and gods of war
Sun god .... Variously the chief god and god of justice
Suwaliyattas .. A warrior god
Takitis .... A male servant god to Hebat
Tasmisus .... A brother and son to Kumarbis
Telepinus .... A fertility god and god of agriculture
Teshub .... Son of Kumarbis a ruler god of many powers including storms
Upelluri .... The giant of a god who supports the world on his back (similar to Atlas)
Ulikummis .... Son of Kumarbis and a mother made of stone.
Uliliyassis ..... A minor god who can correct male impotence
Yarris .... A god of pestilence

Hittite storm god

23
Sumerian/Akkadian Gods

Around 2300-2200 BCE a host of Sumerian gods evolved that tended to personify the natural elements, dangers, and forces that impacted the lives of the people. Typically, each city or region would have its own personalized god or goddess. Over time these gods came to be aligned in a hierarchy of importance and powers and had to be appeased or satisfied with formalized rituals and sacrifice. The real purpose was to join with the gods to have some influence over catastrophic events such as flood, famine, plague, war, drought, and earthquake.

The early villages tended to have a shrine that was set aside for the male and female divinities that were local to that village or region. These shrines tended to be in the form of a storage building for surplus grains or food stocks that would be allocated to the residents throughout the lean periods of the year and a site to pay tribute to the gods. Eventually, with population growth, the shrines evolved into temples and the granary function increased to be a full temple complex or multi-leveled ziggurat.

The broad term "Mesopotamians" refers to groups of early civilizations in the Tigris-Euphrates Valley of what is now primarily the modern nation of Iraq. In addition to many sub-groups over a period of several thousand years and prior to the beginnings of the Christianity, these early people included major groupings of the Sumerians, Akkadians, Babylonians, and Assyrians. The Mesopotamians are often credited with many of the early innovations, such as writing, and moving from a strictly nomadic existence to dwelling in walled cities, and the cultural adaptations that tend to accompany congested lifestyles. Diversification of tasks and inter-dependencies became apparent to survive and prosper against the challenges of nature and roving bands of predatory gangs. New identities and association with a particular place necessitated mutual protection, a sense of order and control, and fledgling development of governing bodies, religion, and trade to meet the people's needs. The record of those early innovations is quite sketchy yet much has survived in the form of written texts and archaeological remains. In that mix of real people experiencing life from birth to death for each individual there was the formation and re-formation of world views and actual survival under frequently difficult circumstances. The world view of the afterlife, for instance, tended to vary and even to be contradictory within that broad region. Typically, the otherworld for Mesopotamians described various levels of immortality for their gods who were exempt from the human condition. For most, the afterlife might be a continuation of day to day existence with continuous search for minimal food and water in a non-descript landscape. The exception for wealthy and powerful individuals was the potential to be accompanied by servants who would provide them with on-going sustenance. Early tombs of noble families have been found that included servants and items thought to be prerequisite for an afterlife. The Mesopotamian underworld did not develop into a place of either reward or punishment but rather a place of featureless space with their gods as overseers. This ill-defined view was also typical of the early Hittites and Canaanites who lived to the west of Mesopotamia. For them, tangible evidence is lacking that death for the common people was anything more than the cessation of life, or perhaps the assumption of a ghost-like spirit. Only later would the perceptions of these people become entwined with the radically different beliefs of the Egyptians, Phoenicians, and the Israelites.

Mesopotamian and Canaanite Gods and Goddesses

Adad .... storm god
Anshar .... Sumerian god of the celestial world
Anu (An) .... father of the gods (god of heaven)
Apsu .... sea god
Ashur .... sky god and principle god of the Assyrians
Baal................... (Ba'al) a lord of heaven
Bel .... god of wisdom and magic
Dagon .... fertility god (Babylonian)
Damu .... god of health and vitality (Sumerian)
Emesh .... god of farmers
Enki (Ea) .... god of earth, air, water, fertility, and wisdom
Enlil .... a ruler god of the air and storms
Erragal .... god of the underworld
Gerra .... god of fire
Gilgamesh.......... Sumerian king who was two parts god and one part human
Inanna .... goddess of love and war (Sumerian)
Irra .... god of plagues
Ishtar................. goddess of love and war (Akkadian)
Ki .... goddess of the earth
Kittu .... god of justice
Marduk .... god-king of Babylon. A god of healing and justice, son of Enki
Nabu .... god of writing and wisdom, son of Marduk
Namtar............... god of death
Nanna .... moon god
Nergal .... god of death
Ninlil.................. goddess of the wind
Sneddon .... food and harvest god
Tiamat .... sea goddess and goddess of chaos
Utu .... sun god

24
Greek Gods and Goddesses

The Greek pantheon of pagan gods and goddesses was very complex. In contrast to the harsh and impersonal gods of the Assyrians and the Babylonians, the Greeks incorporated human qualities along with the supernatural powers of their gods and goddesses. Much of Greek mythology is associated with their gods and blends much material from the Near East, Egypt, Minoan, and other surrounding cultures of antiquity. Greek gods were typically humanoid or superhumans with all of the foibles of ordinary humanity. The entanglements often provided substantial grist for "soap opera" level stories ranging from the trivial to science fiction and beyond. Zeus was the supreme deity and god of the sky. He expressed himself with storms and lightning to show his anger and to administer justice on both heaven and earth.

Most cultures, both ancient and modern, have had strict taboos against incest. There are the obvious genetic complications and the more obvious cultural and legal complications when a father is also an uncle, a grandfather, a brother, or a son. Within Greek mythology and a complex pantheon of gods and goddesses, the supreme deity, Zeus, shared his powers with his siblings. His three brothers and three sisters were all the children of Cronus, his father, by the father's sister, Rhea. Zeus acquired his powers after castrating and overthrowing his father (Cronus) as his father had done with his father before him (Uranus). The male and female deities fathered by Zeus were by different goddesses. To produce a male heir, Zeus looked to his own sisters and eventually produced a daughter, Persephone, by his middle sister, Demeter. Since he still lacked a male heir, Zeus turned to other goddesses. He had nine daughters by Harmonia and then by the goddess Leto, he had both a son and a daughter, known respectively as Apollo and Artemis. Later, Zeus impregnated his own daughter Semele, to produce Dionysus. Obviously, the pressures on the supreme deity to produce heirs by whatever means had its counterpart in the royal house of many monarchies. The mixed message of the ancient world, as conveyed by deities and monarchies, was that women were usually subordinate to men.

Greek Gods and Goddesses

Achilles..........deified hero of the Trojan War
Adephagia......goddess of gluttony
Aeolus............god of winds and storms
Alastor...........god of revenge
Amphitrite.....goddess of the sea
Ananke..........goddess of fate and necessity
Anteros..........god of passion, son of Aphrodite
Antheia..........goddess of flowers
Aphrodite.......goddess of love and beauty, mother of Eros
Apollo............god of music, poetry, and prophecies
Ares...............god of war, son of Zeus
Aristaios........god of herdsmen and hunters
Artemis..........goddess of hunt, wild animals, and moon
Asclepius.......god of healing
Astraea..........goddess of justice, innocence, and purity
Ate.................goddess of foolishness
Athema..........goddess of wisdom, reason, and courage
Attis...............goddess of misfortune, evil, and confusion
Bia.................goddess of force and violence
Boreas...........god of north wind (winter)
Brizo..............goddess of mariners
Calliope.........Greek muse of music and poetry

Carus .... god of luck and good fortune
Cerberus .... guardian of the gates of underworld
Ceto .... goddess of ocean hazards and sea monsters
Charon .... Ferryman for the dead in Hades
Circe .... a powerful witch
Cotys.............. goddess of orgies
Demeter .... goddess of fertility and harvests, sister of
Dionysus .... god of wine, festivities, and drunkenness
Doris .... goddess of the sea, mother of Nereids
Echo .... Greek mountain nymph
Eileithyia .... goddess of childbirth, daughter of Zeus
Elpis .... goddess of hope and expectation
Eos .... goddess of the dawn
Erebus .... god of darkness
Eris .... goddess of discord and strife
Eros .... god of love, sex and fertility
Euros .... god of the east wind
Hades .... god of underworld and the dead, brother of
Hebe .... goddess of youth
Hekate .... goddess of underworld and magic
Helios .... god of the sun
Hemera .... goddess of daylight
Hera .... goddess of marriage, childbirth, and women
Hermes .... god of flight, commerce, and travelers
Hygieia .... goddess of health, and cleanliness
Hymen .... god of marriage, and marital feasts
Hyperion .... god of light
Hypnos .... god of sleep
Mania .... goddess of insanity
Metis .... goddess of wisdom, first wife of Zeus
Moira .... the Greek fates
Momos .... god of satire, criticism, and blame

Morpheus	god of dreams
Muses	goddesses of arts and sciences
Nemesis	goddess of retribution, justice, and vengeance
Nereus	god of the sea "Old Man of the Sea"
Nike	goddess of victory
Notus	god of the south wind
Pan	god of shepherds, pastures, and fertility
Peitho	goddess of seduction and persuasion
Persephone	goddess of earth's fertility and underworld
Poseidon	god of the sea, earthquakes, and storms
Priapus	god of male virility, son of Aphrodite
Proteus	god of the sea "Old Man of the Sea"
Satyr	half-man, half-goat spirit god of woods
Selene	goddess of the moon
Sirens	half bird-gods, half women
Thanatos	god of death
Thetis	daughter of sea god, mother of Achilles
Titans	rebellious lesser gods
Triton	minor sea god, Poseidon's messenger
Typhon	whirlwind god, monster god
Uranus	god of the heavens
Zephyrus	god of the west wind
Zephyrus	goddess of the west wind
Zeus	king of gods, sky, thunder, all powerful

Zeus

25
Roman Gods and Goddesses

Traditional Roman religion focused on rituals that were performed publicly by representatives of the state, or privately within the individual family. As in most pagan religions, the relationship between Romans and their gods was fairly close, personal, and something of a contractual agreement. Romans satisfied the bond they had with particular gods through prescribed rituals, offerings, and sacrifices intended to give them good fortune and protection from the potentially negative elements of daily life. By the third century BCE, Roman gods acquired a more human form when the Greek pantheon of gods was absorbed into their essentially pragmatic belief systems. The three most significant gods were the triad of Jupiter (Zeus), Juno (Hera), and Minerva (Athene). Roman gods were modeled after or simply adopted from the Greek pantheon of gods and goddesses. In addition, there was a broad range of household gods and goddesses that were highly regarded. Various cults existed that tended to have different emphases, but most shared the belief in a judgment after death where the individual would either be saved or damned throughout eternity.

Ancient Roman religious traditions were pervasive throughout all of the social classes and tended to be a combination of tolerant and even cult-oriented. A broad range of deities, beliefs, and behaviors were tolerated to the extent that there was not an open conflict with official Roman traditions, laws, and customs. As a result of being a far-flung empire, the Roman people were in a position of assumed superiority and were tolerant of diverse beliefs from wide-ranging sources that did not conflict with the Roman sense of order, law, and preservation of the empire. It was exclusivity, the belief in one god to the exclusion of all others, that offended Roman administrators the most. Gods were openly borrowed from the provinces and Romanized. Cults of many different kinds, including mystery cults, were tolerated. It was among the patrician classes, however, that limits were set. Sustained efforts were made to repress perceived conflicts in beliefs by the harshest methods deemed necessary. Following the sack of Jerusalem in 70 CE, for example, large numbers of Jewish prisoners of war were deported to Rome to build the coliseum and settlements in the region were allowed. Just 20-miles west of Rome, the Port of Rome, Ostia Antiqua, was massively rebuilt under the supervision of Emperor Hadrian and eventually had a Jewish Synagogue. During the years of 387 to 388 CE, however, that synagogue was destroyed by Christian mobs. By 391 CE, the last Roman emperor of both east and west, Theodosius I, proclaimed that all pagan temples were to be closed and pagan worship was forbidden. Far from being deified himself, Theodosius would see the division of the Roman Empire into east and west. Western Roman emperors may have assumed some of the trappings of a deity, but it was with Constantine, founder of the Eastern Roman Empire at Constantinople, who began to see themselves as god-like.

Roman Gods and Goddesses

Amor .... god of love (Gr Eros)
Bacchus .... god of wine and drunkenness (Gr Dionysos)
Carmenta .... goddess of fate and fortune (Gr Themis)
Ceres .... goddess of corn harvest (Gr Demeter)
Concordia ...... goddess of peace and harmony
Cupid .... god of love (Gr Eros)
Diana .... goddess of moon and woodlands (Gr Artemis)
Discordia .... goddess of strife (Gr Eris)

Fauna	goddess of fertility and nature
Felicitas	goddess of happiness and good fortune
Flora	goddess of flowers and blossoms
Fortuna	goddess of fate and chance
Genita-Mana	god with power of life and death
Genius	a protective god
Janus	god of beginnings, endings, and transitions
Juno	chief goddess of women (Gr Hera)
Jupiter	chief god of sky, light, thunder and power (Gr Zeus)
Lacturna	goddess of wheat crop
Lemurs	god of evil
Mars	god of war (Gr Ares)
Mellonia	goddess of bees & honey
Minerva	goddess of war (Etruscan Menrva)
Mutinus	god of fertility
Neptune	god of the sea (Gr Poseidon)
Orcus	god of the underworld (Gr Thanatos)
Pax	goddess of peace (Gr Eirene)
Pluto	god of the underworld
Portunus	god of gates and harbors
Providentia	goddess of forethought
Saturn	god of agriculture (Gr Kronos)
Scabie	god associated with skin rashes
Sol	sun god (Gr Helios)
Tellus	earth goddess (Gr Cybele)
Vacuna	goddess of leisure
Venus	goddess of love and beauty (Gr Aphrodite)
Vesper	god of the night
Vesta	goddess of the hearth and fire
Virtus	god of courage and military might
Vulcan	god of fire (Gr Hephaistos)

Predecessors to the Roman deities were the Etruscan gods and goddesses represented as Alpan, Ani, Aplu, Aritimi, Atunis, Castur and Pultuce, Cautha, Charontes, Charun, Culsu, Februus, Feronia, Fufluus, Genii, Horta, Kamenae, Larau, Lasas, Laverna, Liber, Libera, Mania, Mater Matuta, Menrvaa, Nethuus, Nortia, Selvanus, Sethlaus, Summanus, Tages, Thalna, Thesan, Tinia, Tuchulcha, Tura, Turms, Uni, Vanth, Vediovis, Veive, Voltumna, and Volta.

Jupiter image at a fountain in Rome

Roman Forum

Roman Coliseum

26
Scandinavian Gods and Goddesses

Unlike ancient Greek gods, where older and younger families of gods were in competition, such as the Titans versus the Olympians, Norse gods existed in major and minor clans that were contemporaneous with each other. The major clan was known as Aesir and the minor clan was Vanir. Their broad range of activities paralleled their human counterparts on a grander mythological scale. The Norse Vikings (including Norway, Sweden, Denmark, Iceland, and northern Germanic territories) believed in a pantheon of gods who had origins in Germanic Indo-European culture. The primary god was Odin, a father-figure and lord of magic. He was the god of the underworld and the afterlife. Among his followers were the Berserkers. It was their crazed, wild animal-like behavior in battle that has given us a term that is associated with all-out, screaming madman attacks in times of war. Odin's son, Thor, did not possess the omniscient powers of his father but was more popular with the people. Thor was represented as a very powerful figure who traveled across the skies in a chariot and was noted for his fearful temper and superhuman strength. The Scandinavian god of fertility was called Freyr. He was the son of Njord, who was the god of ships and of the sea. The Vanir clan represented a group of gods that were associated with the sea and the land. The opposing group, the more powerful Aesir clan, represented gods of the sky.

Their inclusion here, with Eastern Mediterranean gods, relates to one of the last stages of European paganism in the form of virtually unstoppable Viking raids on Europe, from the east coast of England to Paris, France, to Moscow, and beyond. The first

Loki, the Nordic god of change, as a satyr

Viking raid was a devastating attack on a defenseless English monastery at Lindisfarne in 793 CE. Those assaults and indifference to fledgling Christianity, with a potential to spread Nordic paganism, did not subside until 911 CE when the king of the West Franks, Charles the Simple, granted the Viking invaders the province of Normandy as a peace settlement. By 1066 CE, William the Conqueror of Normandy attacked southeastern England with the blessings of the Catholic Church, but no longer as a Viking. The French Norman invasion followed the failed attempt to invade and conquer Northern England by the Viking forces of the self-proclaimed King Harald Hardrada.

The greatest threat to fledgling Christianity was the seemingly unstoppable spread of Islam following the death of Muhammad, the Prophet of Islam, in 632 CE. The Islamic faith had spread throughout much of the Middle East, Northern Africa, and the Iberian Peninsula of Western Europe. Other religions were tolerated in the occupied areas, and the militant forces of Islam fully intended to capture all of France and beyond. Instead, those forces were confronted by King Charles "the Hammer" Martel at the Battle of Tours in 732 CE and the Islamic advance further into Europe was stopped. Finally, by 1492, King Ferdinand and Queen Isabella of Spain joined forces to evict the Moors from that country.

Nordic Gods and Goddesses

Aegir .... god of the sea
Aesir Clan ...... includes Odin, Frigg, Thor, Balder and Tyr
Andvari .... god of guarded treasures
Balder .... son of Odin and Frigg, an Aesir Clan god
Beowulf .... Anglo-Saxon hero. He fights monster, Grendl, in an epic poem
Bragi .... god of poetry (married to Idun)
Forseti .... god of justice, son of Balder and Nanna
Freya .... goddess of love, fertility, beauty, and creativity, sister of Freyja
Freyr .... god of weather and fertility
Frigg .... goddess of love & fertility, wife of Odin, mother of Balder, Hod and Hermod
Gefn .... goddess of gift-giving
Heimdall .... god of light, a protector god
Hod .... blind god of winter, son of Odin who accidentally kills his brother, Balder
Idun .... goddess of eternal youth

Iduna .... goddess of the underworld, immortality
Loki .... trickster god, magician, potentially evil prankster
Mimir .... a guardian god of the well of wisdom
Nanna .... goddess/wife of Balder who dies of grief following Balder's death
Njord .... god of the wind and sea
Odin .... the father of all gods (war, death, and wisdom), father of Thor by Jord
Sif .... wife of Thor (has elements of Rumplestilskin in her story)
Thor .... god of thunder, a chief god, son of Odin (Thursday is named after Thor)
Tyr .... god of war and justice who lost his right hand to the giant wolf, Fenrir
Vanir Clan ...... includes Njord, Freyer, Freyja
Ve .... god and brother of Odin
Vili .... god and brother of Odin

Viking Museum, Oslo, Norway

Aztec Gods

In stark contrast to the religion and mythology that originated near the banks of the eastern Mediterranean, the people of Meso-America prior to the arrival of the first Europeans had what amounted to no contact with the world outside of their immediate region. The parallels of beliefs in religion and mythology were strikingly similar to Old World paganism. For the Aztec people, religion, art, architecture, and rich cultural stories were very much a central focus of their lives. Within that totality of beliefs and cultural inventions was a focus on agricultural gods and festivities because their very existence was so dependent on successful farming and everything related to it. The mysteries of the natural world were thus in the realm of the gods. Therefore, special thanks and acknowledgements had to be expressed in a wide variety of ways that took on very serious aspects of the sacred and inviolate. Ceremonial rituals to honor the specific gods were marked by sacrifices that culminated in the greatest sacrifice of all ritual human sacrifice to obtain the favorable blessings of the gods.

Aztec Gods and Goddesses

Centeotl .... god of corn
Chalchiuhtlicue ... goddess of lakes and streams
Chantico .... goddess of volcanoes and fires
Chicomecoatl ...... goddess of fertility and the harvest
Cihuacoatyl .... goddess of maternity and motherhood
Contlicue .... goddess mother of earth, moon, and stars
Coyolxauhqui ...... moon goddess
Ehecatl .... wind god
Huitzilopochtli .... god of war and successful harvests
Ixtlilton .... god of healing
Metztli .... god of moon and darkness

Mictecacihuatl ..... goddess of underworld
Mictlantecuhtle ... god of the dead
Mixcoatl .... god of the hunt
Nanahuatzin .... Sun god
Nanauatzin .... god of sacrifice
Omacatl .... god of feasting and joy
Patecatli .... god of healing
Paynal .... god of deception
Quetzalcoatl .... the principle creator god.
Tecciztecatl .... moon god
Teoyaomqu .... god of dead warriors
Teoyaomqui .... god of deceased warriors
Tepeyyollotl .... god of earthquakes
Tepoztecatl .... god of fertility and drunkenness
Tezcatlipoca .... god of the night, temptation, war, and magic
Tlaloc .... god of rain and fertility
Tloqunahuaque ... a creator god, god of mystery and the unknown
Tonatiuh .... sun god
Xochipilli .... god of love
Xochiquetzal .... goddess of beauty
Xolotl .... god of the underworld and misfortune

Aztec solar calendar

Conclusion

Recently, Tibet's exiled spiritual leader, the Dalai Lama, warned his followers that Tibetan culture, religion, and identity face extinction, and he described current realities for native residents of Tibet as a "hell on earth." These comments, made by a Nobel Prize-winning pacifist, were contained in a speech made to acknowledge the fiftieth anniversary of a failed Tibetan uprising. Such is the current legacy of an ancient culture bordering on the sacred in the highlands of the Himalayan Mountains that is being absorbed, as if by an enormous amoeba, by another culture that is vastly superior in strength and numbers. It also reflects an enormously tragic story of domination and forced assimilation of one cultural group by another throughout human history. The dominant culture often absorbs and incorporates random elements of the oppressed culture, but in too many instances, such as Native American examples, entire cultures, histories, mythologies, religions, and even languages were irrevocably lost. It is a major premise of this book that fanatical extremes associated with the three great religions that formed near the banks of the Eastern Mediterranean that focus on any one belief as the only true belief robs us all of the diversity and richness of humanity's potential.

When Genghis Khan's superior military strategies and unstoppable forces annihilated entire villages to the extent that there was not a tear left to be shed for the deceased, he erased all that had ever been accomplished, discovered, or recorded within that village. It was like erasing all that the Tibetan people have given to the world and to each other for countless generations. When the Spanish adventurer, Juan Ponce de Leon, pursued a paramilitary quest through the region that was to become Florida and the Southeastern United States, there was a slim chance that he was in search of the fabled "Fountain of Youth." The most probable motivation was the acquisition of tangible riches and personal fame. What his forces introduced, however, was European diseases that annihilated entire cultures that had thousands of years of life experiences that could no longer be passed on in some positive way. Native Americans were typically religious people with a firm concept of the afterlife, god(s), creation stories, and life experiences that ran the gamut of birth to death for untold generations. The Spanish conquistadors who encountered surviving elements of the Mayan culture were so offended by the likelihood that human sacrifice to the gods had been practiced as a part of their religion that the conquistadors burned virtually all of the recorded history of that unique and highly sophisticated population of Native Americans. It is a narrow-minded anti-intellectual who believes there is just one interpretation of religion and cultural rightness or wrongness.

Oral and written material that has been handed down for thousands of years, composed and recomposed repeatedly by unknown authors and scribes, and subjected to multiple translations is certain to be something less than the absolute literal word of God. It was the intent of the European Inquisition to preserve Catholicism. Yet the result of the over-zealous methods applied was one of the darkest periods in human history. The tragedy of religious overzealousness and alien microbes especially impacted millions of Native Americans who occupied one-third of the world's habitable space in relative isolation for thousands of years and had their own religious beliefs and traditions. Virtually all of their life and death experiences and everything in between has been lost. The abrupt displacement of thousands of years of Egyptian religious beliefs by a single pharaoh, Akhenaten, over 1,300 years before the birth of Christ, was met with disbelief, virtual civil war, murder, and quick re-establishment of the old gods. The living God of Abraham and Moses has been described as a loving God, but also as a jealous and vindictive God who all but destroyed the world with a great flood, wildfires, eruptions, droughts, earthquakes, and disease. At times the issues were just petty, such as denying Moses the right to set foot on the Promised Land because he performed a water-producing miracle by the method that had not been pre-approved by God. Moses was clearly competing with dominant cultures on all sides that were committed to a long-standing world of pagan gods and goddesses. His own followers reverted to belief in paganism in the historical/biblical record. There are, in fact, parallels between Moses and the heretical pharaoh, Akhenaten, that have pushed some scholars, including Sigmund Freud, to believe that Moses and Akhenaten could possibly be one and the same individual. Additional purposes of this book have been to chronologically separate these two historical/biblical giants by more than 200 years and to reconfirm that Moses was the most effective progenitor of a more universal form of monotheism after the patriarchal family of Abraham, Isaac, and Jacob. The heretic pharaoh, Akhenaten, entered the world's stage over two centuries after Moses and can be considered a convert of his Semitic maternal grandparents, Joseph and his wife (Yuya and Thuya). Akhenaten, the heretic pharaoh, cannot be the unnamed pharaoh who was influenced centuries earlier by a man named Joseph of the Many-Colored Coat. That Joseph may have either become Moses, or pre-dated the biblical Moses and yet was a significant influence on the actual leader of the Exodus around the time of 1600 BCE.

The historical transcendence from regional gods and goddesses that was very much ingrained in the pagan world to a universal living God can be largely attributed to Moses and his devout Israelite followers who were re-absorbed into Canaanite culture and territories over a period of approximately four centuries following Joshua's over-embellished invasion of the ancient city of Jericho. A cultural re-absorption that takes up to 400 years is not the same as the violent and bloody conquest by force that has so often been portrayed. Instead, based upon linguistic, cultural, and archeological evidence, there is very good reason to believe that a minority sect of Canaanites, who were the non-pagan followers of Abraham, Isaac, and Jacob, evolved into the Hebrew/Israelite/Jewish people of that region and of the northeastern Delta lands of Egypt. The Canaanite people who had accepted pagan gods were ultimately absorbed by the fiercely tenacious minority of Hebrews, Israelites, and Jews, who, like the Hyksos people, were all descendants of the broad pool of Semitic people dating back to at least 2,000-3,000 BCE. The tragic irony of their geo-political positioning in the region of present-day Israel is that these hardy people would be oppressed and at times dislocated by vastly more powerful neighbors including the Egyptians, Hittites, Sumerians, Babylonians, Phoenicians/Philistines, Hyksos, Greeks, Romans, and perhaps other Mideastern invaders now lost to history. The culturally sustaining and binding forces of these often oppressed people living in the narrow crossroads of ancient history were the exclusivity and fierceness of their belief in one true living God while surrounded by a fluctuating mishmash of pagan idol worshipers.

Paganism and the almost inseparable mythology that sustains it has been mankind's primary solution to the deep dark questions associated with daily living. Where did we come from? Why do bad things happen to good people? Where do we go when we die? What are the causes and the possible solutions to tragic events such as floods, volcanic eruptions, droughts, disease, earthquakes, infertility, wars, pestilence, violence, deceit, and all of the questions that arise from the time a child first learns to speak and to interact with the surrounding world? Can we, as individuals or members of groups, influence our environment in positive ways, or, as Shakespeare once commented in *King Lear* (Act 4, Scene 1), "As flies to wanton boys, are we to the gods. They kill us for their sport." Can science reconcile more and more of the gulf between faith and factual documentation and the potential to confirm reality by proofs that can be replicated, measured, dated, and objectively confirmed with a high level of confidence and general acceptance? Is there an everlasting life after death? If so, how can it ever be confirmed and understood when there is no scientific basis for resurrection from the dead and a blissful immortality except as a brief medical fluke, or the word of someone who claims to have experienced an aura of white light beyond death? Is it not possible that the concept of an immortal afterlife has been oversold on the basis that it cannot be verified one way or the other with any degree of scientific proof and consensus? What are the true criteria for attaining immortality, and is there a St. Peter standing at the gate, or a similar mechanism, for making determinations about who receives either a positive or a negative immortality? Dante's Inferno tried to quantify different levels and degrees for a negative immortality in a poetic, mythological way. Has anyone run the numbers lately? Tens of billions of souls experiencing an irrevocable immortality are going to occupy a very large universe where overlap with all of one's ancestors based on age at the time of death will not be what the Egyptian pharaohs anticipated based on their funerary records and tomb paintings. Is it possible that immortality has been oversold on the basis that it is a positive answer to the trauma and permanent separation of death and cannot be verified one way or the other? Can we anticipate sharing eternal paradise with possibly billions and billions of others who don't speak our language and who share none of our life's experiences? Does our prehistoric ancestor dating back from 10,000 to 1,000,000 years really have anything in common with us, or does that person just want a perpetual good meal and a dry place to sleep forever?

The common thread of paganism is to attribute responsibility for much of what happens on this very unique and special planet to some superhuman deity. The more humane gods and goddesses often shared many of the foibles and weaknesses of their human counterparts, but always had some superpower that could be used in a positive, negative, or irresponsible way.

The issues of personal responsibility for our actions and a high level of care for others who happen to share our contemporaneous world have actually been lessened by a reliance on the capriciousness and mysteriousness of the actions of the gods. Man's inhumanity to man has often been attributed to a disregard for the gods, or a feeling that God is on the side of the prevailing group. Acceptance by a benign and loving God who can accept each and every one of us (well, almost all of us) in a perpetual state of unconditional love is something to be truly ecstatic about and to focus our energies on attaining. The Calvinists imagined that some people would be accepted into such a state of grace pretty much at random. Other sources have tried to apply other criteria. A few have even suggested that a sacrificial human bomber can anticipate spending eternity with 42 to 72 virgins. Mostly, humans, with a true respect for other humans, want to be reunited with recently predeceased relatives and friends. The twist with that particular ideal is that eternity will be ageless and timeless, yet each of us will die at different ages. Consider someone who dies at a very advanced age whose parents died when that person was just a small child. All conceivable variations are possible. Another random notion is that every person will advance either forward or backward to the ideal age of thirty years to spend eternity together. For the Egyptian pharaoh it was enough to return to the relative paradise of ancient Egypt with all of the affluence, power, and privilege that he enjoyed while alive.

It is language more than religion, economics, or any other single factor that has done the most to differentiate humans from all other species on this planet; including chimpanzees, who have approximately 95% of the same DNA as humans. Therefore, based on tracing the evolution of languages and DNA that can be reliably followed back 50,000 years and more, the migrations and perhaps even the ethnicities of most of the world's larger groupings of people can be identified with some degree of certainty. The downside of linguistic tracking is that language extinction has been occurring for at least 10,000 years as a result of transfer from nomadic hunting and gleaning to agriculture. It has been reported by Living Tongues Institute for Endangered Languages (a non-profit organization partnering with National Geographic) that, prior to the advent of widespread agriculture, there were countless languages with a limited geographic sphere, but as agriculture allowed human settlements to concentrate and expand, languages began to merge and others became extinct. The current reality is that Mandarin, English, Russian, Arabic, Spanish, and to a much lesser extent, German, French, Cantonese, and Italian, will continue to advance in dominating most of the world's languages. Effective February, 2009, UNESCO initiated an online atlas of endangered languages and reported that roughly 2,400 languages are at risk of extinction. It has been estimated by research groups that roughly half of the estimated 7,000 remaining languages in the world will be extinct by 2100-2125. The rapidly accelerating decline of the world's unique languages is a very harsh reality for countless native speakers, yet each and every language, like each and every human who ever existed on this planet, is not guaranteed immortality, except on the basis of personal faith. The quest to raise humanity to a higher plane one person at a time will grow with tolerance of inclusiveness, not fanatic adherence to dogma. The essence of nature for the early pagans that made up most of human history was typically focused on four elements fire (including sunlight), earth, water, and air (wind/storms). From earliest pre-scientific times, an infinite diversity of beliefs and attitudes have evolved from those few elements combined with human interactions.

Author's background Karl C. Hendricksen has been a resident of the Pacific Northwest for over 50 years. He has been an independent spirit with careers in social service and sales and has been an eclectic observer of the human condition from earliest origins to the present.

St. Patrick (c. 387-460) facilitated the conversion of Irish pagans to Christianity by allowing the symbolism of the sun to be incorporated with the cross.

Bibliography

Ahmed Osman, *Moses and Akhenaten: The Secret History of Egypt at the Time of the Exodus* (Rochester, Vermont, Bear & Company, 1990, 2002).

Albert Hourani, *A History of the Arab Peoples* (Cambridge, MA, 1991).

Alessandro Bongioanni and Maria Sole Croce, Editors, *The Treasures of Ancient Egypt The Collection of the Egyptian Museum in Cairo* (Vercelli, Italy, VMB Publishers, 2003).

Benjamin R. Foster and Karen Polinger Foster, *Civilizations of Ancient Iraq* (New Jersey, Princeton University Press, 2009).

Brian M. Fagan, *Return to Babylon Travelers, Archaeologists, and Monuments in Mesopotamia* Boulder, CO, University Press of Colorado, 2007).

Brian M. Fagan, *The Seventy Great Mysteries of the Ancient World Unlocking the Secrets of Past Civilizations* (London, Thames & Hudson, Ltd., 2001).

Brian Hayden, *Archaeology The Science of Once and Future Things* (New York, W. H. Freeman and Company, 1993).

David W. Anthony, *The Horse, The Wheel, and Language How Bronze-Age Riders from the Eurasian Steppes Shaped the Modern World* (Princeton, NJ, Princeton University Press, 2007).

Deepak Chopra, *Life After Death The Burden of Proof* (New York, Harmony Books, 2006).

Dr. William Spencer, *Global Studies The Middle East*, 9th Edition (Guilford, CT, McGraw-Hill, 2003).

Dr. Zahi Hawass, et al., *History and Faith Cradle & Crucible in the Middle East* (Washington, D.C., National Geographic Society, 2002).

E. A. Wallis Budge, *The Egyptian Book of the Dead The Papyrus of Ani* (New York, Dover Publications, Inc., 1967).

E. A. Wallis Budge, *The Gods of the Egyptians Studies in Egyptian Mythology*, Vol. 1 (New York, Dover Publications, Inc., 1969).

Francis Robinson, Editor, *The Cambridge Illustrated History of the Islamic World* (London, Cambridge University Press, 1996).

Furio Durando, *White State Guides Archaeology Greece Vercelli, Italy*, White Star, 2004)

Giovanna Magi, *Abu Simbel Aswan and the Nubian Temples* (Florence, Italy, Casa Editrice Bonechi, 2007).

Goran Burenhult, Editor, *The First Humans Human Origins and History to 10,000 BC* (New York, HarperCollins, 1993).

Graham Clark, *World Prehistory in New Perspective*, 3rd Edition (London, Cambridge University Press, 1977).

Graham Hancock, *Underworld The Mysterious Origins of Civilization* (New York, Three Rivers Press, 2002).

Gwendolyn Endicott, *The Spinning Wheel The Art of Mythmaking* (Portland, OR, Attic Press, 1994).

H.V.F. Winstone, *Uncovering the Ancient World* (London, Constable & Company, Ltd., 1985).

Helen Strudwick, *The Encyclopedia of Ancient Egypt* (London, Amber Books, Ltd., 2007, 2008).

I. E. S. Edwards, *Tutankhamun His Tomb and Its Treasures* (New York, The Metropolitan Museum of Art & Alfred A. Knopf, Inc., 1976).

J. G. MacQueen, *The Hittites and Their Contemporaries in Asia Minor* (London, Thames & Hudson, Ltd., 1975, 1986).

Jack Finegan, *Light from the Ancient Past The Archaeological Background of Judaism and Christianity*, Volume 1 (New Jersey, Princeton University Press, 1974).

Jared Diamond, *Guns, Germs, and Steel: The Fates of Human Societies* (New York, W. W. Norton & Company, 1997, 1999).

Jared Diamond, *The Third Chimpanzee The Evolution and Future of the Human Animal* (New York, Harper Perennial, 1992).

Jean Paul Barbier, *Vanished Civilizations From the Ancients to Easter Island* (New York, Assouline Publishing, Inc., 2001).

Jean Seznec, *The Survival of the Pagan Gods The Mythological Tradition and Its Place in Renaissance Humanism and Art* (New York, Harper Torchbooks, 1953, 1961).

Jim Marrs, *Rule by Secrecy: The Hidden History that Connects the Trilateral Commission, the Freemasons, and the Great Pyramids* (New York, HarperCollins Publishers, Inc., 2000).

John A. Gowlett, *Ascent to Civilization The Archaeology of Early Man* (New York, Alfred A. Knopf, 1984).

Joseph Campbell, *The Power of Myth with Bill Moyers* (New York, Doubleday, 1988).

Josephine Bacon, *The Illustrated Atlas of Jewish Civilization 4000 Years of History* (London, Quantum Books, 1990).

Kate Santon, *Archaeology Unearthing the Mysteries of the Past* (Bath, UK, Parragon Publishing, 2007).

Kathryn A. Bard, *An Introduction to the Archaeology of Ancient Egypt* (Oxford, Blackwell Publishing, 2008).

Kenneth Clark, *Animals and Men* (New York, William Morrow and Company, Inc., 1977).

Kenneth L. Feder, *Frauds, Myths, and Mysteries Science and Pseudoscience in Archaeology*, 6th Edition (Boston, McGraw-Hill Higher Education, 1990, 2001, 2008).

Linda Blandford and Peter Davidson, *Milestones of Civilization* (London, New Holland Publishers, 2009).

Lorna Oakes and Lucia Gahlin, *Ancient Egypt An Illustrated Reference to the Myths, Religions, Pyramids and Temples of the Land of the Pharaohs* (London, Hermes House, 2002, 2008).

Lucia Gahlin, *Egypt Gods, Myths and Religion* (London, Anness Publishing, 2001).

Mohamed Nasr and Mario Tosi, *The Tomb of Nefertari* (Florence, Italy, Casa Editrice Bonechi, 2004).

National Geographic.com/Magazine (Washington, D.C., National Geographic Society).

Nicolas Grimal, *A History of Ancient Egypt* (Oxford, UK, Blackwell Publishers, 1988, 1994).

Nicholas Reeves, *Akhenaten Egypt's False Prophet* (London, Thames & Hudson, Ltd., 2001).

Nina Burleigh, *Unholy Business: A True Tale of Faith, Greed & Forgery in the Holy Land* (New York, HarperCollins Publishers, 2008).

Obery M. Hendricks, Jr., *The Politics of Jesus: Rediscovering the True Revolutionary Nature of Jesus' Teachings and How They Have Been Corrupted* (New York, Doubleday, 2006).

Paul Collins, *From Egypt to Babylon: The International Age 1550-500 BC* (Cambridge Harvard University Press, 2008).

Philip Wilkinson, *Myths & Legends: An Illustrated Guide to Their Origins and Meanings* (London, DK London, 2009).

R.J. Hopper, *The Early Greeks* (New York, Harper & Row Publishers, Inc., 1976).

Robert S. Bianchi, *Splendors of Ancient Egypt* (London, Booth-Clibbon Editions, 1996).

Robin Lane Fox, *Pagans and Christians* (New York, Alfred A. Knopf, 1986).

Ruth Whitehouse and John Wilkins, *The Making of Civilization History Discovered Through Archaeology* (New York, Alfred A. Knopf, 1988).

Stephen Bertman, *Handbook to Life in Ancient Mesopotamia* (New York, Oxford University Press, 2003).

The Holy Bible New Revised Standard Version (Grand Rapids, Michigan, Zondervan, 1989).

Thomas H. Flaherty, Editor, *The Spirit World Alexandria, VA*, Time-Life Books, 1992).

Zecharia Sitchin, *The 12th Planet* (New York, Avon Books, 1976).

Cave painting, Lascaux, France, c. 15,000-30,0000 BCE

Journey Up the Nile

In 2008, this writer had the rare opportunity to travel upstream on portions of the world's longest river from Cairo, Egypt to the southern reaches of Lake Nasser and monuments of Abu Simbel. The experience of being in such close proximity with more than 5,000 years of human evolution and development along the Nile River was mesmerizing.

Cairo city view

View of the Nile from Marriott King Farouk Palace Hotel, Cairo

Additional Cairo city view

The Citadel and Mohammad Ali Mosque, Cairo

Temple of Luxor

Outside alabaster factory near the Valley of the Kings

Avenue of the Ram-Headed Sphinxes at Karnak

Seated statues of Ramesses II at a gate (pylon) of the Temple of Luxor

Obolisk located in the Temple of Luxor

Deeply cut cartouche on column in the Hypostyle Hall at Karnak

Sample hieroglyphics at the Temple of Karnak

Temple of Hatshepsut near the Valley of the Kings

Closer view of a portion of the Temple of Hatshepsut, the female pharaoh

The Colossi of Memnon (statue of Amenhotep III)

Colossi of Memnon forming gate to Amenhotep's funerary temple

Sailboat on the Nile in the style of an ancient felucca

Temple of Philae from the Nile

Mausoleum of Agha Khan up the bank from the Nile

Temple of Philae

Temple of Kalabsha with lotus-style tribute to Russian Friendship in background

Detail of Kalbsha (a Nubian Temple built during the Ptolemaic Period)

Abu Simbel

Abu Simbel statue of Ramesses II

Abu Simbel tribute to Queen Nefertari

Abu Simbel

Mammoth statue of Ramesses II, the Colossus of Memphis

The step pyramid of Djoser at Saqqara (c. 2667 to 2648 BCE)

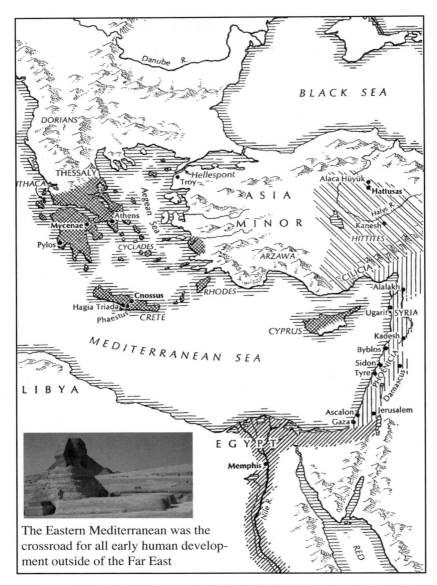

The Eastern Mediterranean was the crossroad for all early human development outside of the Far East

Asia Minor at the time of the Trojan War c.1250 BCE. Reprinted from Jay Kimmel's *50 Battles: 5,000 Years of Conflict*, by permission.

Index

Aaron 45, 51, 128
Abraham 27-9, 53, 107-110, 129
Abu Simbel 26, 75
Abydos 75
Achilles 5
Adam and Eve 142-3
Adikam 43
afterlife 8, 23-4, 35, 147
Ahmose 43, 56
Ahura Mazda 112
Akhenaten 43, 65, 72, 77-8, 80-2, 109
Akkadian 27, 30
Amarna kings 85
Amarna Period 81, 87, 91
Amenhotep III 71
Amenhotep IV 73
Ammonite 30
Amun 97
Anatolia 44, 163
ancient ancestors 11
ancient burial sites 11
angry Horus 10, 96
Ankhesenamun 83, 167
Anubis 154
Arab Christian faithful 119
Arabic language 33
Aramaic 27, 30-1, 117, 121
Ark of the Covenant 49-50
Armstrong, Karen 109
Assyrian 39
Aten 74, 77, 85
Atlantis 7
australopithecines 14, 19
Avaris 38-9, 75
Aye 72, 75, 78, 89, 97, 99
Baal 114

Babylon 27, 30, 114, 117
Batman 6
Battle of Milvia 125
Battle of Tours 185
Berserkers 183
Bronze Age 17, 47, 57
Cain and Abel 134, 144
Canaan 30
Canaanite language 33
Carbon-14 11, 19
cartouches 96
cast the first stone 120
Chaldeans 30
chaos 22, 42
chariots 37
Chichen Itza 138
chimpanzees 14
Christianity 110
civilization 16
Cleopatra 77
Colossi of Memnon 71, 209, 210
comparative ancient gods 105
Coptic Christians 90
Council of Nicea 126
cradle of civilization 27, 76
crucifixion 116, 122, 165
crystal ball reader 127
cuneiform 11
Cyrus II 114
Dalai Lama 189
Dark Ages 132
Darwin, Charles 7
Dead Sea scrolls 110, 115
decomposition 22
Diamond, Jared 16
Diaspora 118
divine energy 12

divine intervention 12
DNA 19, 73, 81, 86, 94, 96, 195
domestic animals 16
droughts 21
Duchesne, Ernest 21
Eber 108
Edfu Temple 10
Elijah 114
Emperor Augustus 122
Emperor Constantine 124, 179
emperor of Ethiopia 112
Emperor Theodosius 125, 179
end times 117
Essenes 121
eternity 23
everlasting life 23
Exodus 36-7, 39, 42, 111
expulsion of Hyksos 40
eye of a needle 120
false prophet 124, 128
fertility gods 20
Five Pillars of Faith 130
floods 21
folklore 8-9, 27
Freud, Sigmund 90, 93, 191
Froehlich's Syndrome 81, 86
Gabriel 130
Galilee 116
Geb 12
Genghis Khan 189
Gibbons, Ann 14
Gilgamesh 44
Giza 34
Goshen 40, 44-5, 75, 111
gospels 124
Green Hornet 6
Gutenberg, Johann 8
Hagar 28, 100
Hajj 131

Hammurabi 165
Haran 28, 107
Hattusili I 163
Hawass, Zahi 18-9, 83, 86, 92
Hebrew god 52
Hebrews 30, 108
Heliopolis 12, 56, 92
Herod 44
Hieroglyphs 11
Hittites 33, 36, 44, 163-70
homo erectus 14
Horemheb 74, 85, 89, 91, 99-104
Horus 38
Howard, Gen. O.O. 46
Hyksos 36-7
Ice Age 21
immortality 23-4
infant mortality 13, 123
infections 18
intelligence 14, 19
invasion of Canaan 30
Iraq 27
iron oxide 57
Isaac 48, 53, 107, 129
Isaiah 114-15
Ishmael 28, 108, 129
Ishmaelites 108
Islam 110, 112, 129-32
Israel 115
Israelites 53, 107-08, 111, 115, 122
Jacob 48, 53, 107-08, 110
Jacobovici, Simcha 57
JAMA 43, 73, 86
Jebel el-Lawz 50
Jericho 16, 48, 67-8, 192
Jerusalem 117
Jesus Christ 30, 94, 116-7, 120
Jewish scripture 127
John the Baptist 116

Joseph 63-6
Joseph (Yuya) 65-6, 71, 77-9, 85, 88
Joshua 48
Judah 114
Judaism 110
Kadesh 98, 168
Khendjer 36
Khufu 23
Khyan 40
King Charles Martel 185
King David 112, 115
King Lear 193
King Solomon 112
Kohler disease 84
Koran (Qur'an) 130
Krakatoa 55
kryptonite 5
Kush 75
Lake Nyos 57
Lazarus 124
Leakey, Richard 19
Libya 47
lifespans 19
Lincoln, Abraham 7
linguists 11
Lloyd, Allen 71
locusts 59
Lot 28
Lucy 19
magic 22
male circumcision 33
Malul 43
Manetho 92
Marfan's Syndrome 81, 86
mastabas 23, 35
Mayan glyphs 11
Memphis 12, 19, 75
Mesopotamia 31, 106-07, 171
messiah 116, 120, 123

microscope 20
Middle Kingdom 34
Middle Ages 118, 124, 167
Midianites 47
Mighty Mouse 6
Miles, Gen. Nelson 46
Minoans 33, 55
Miriam 128
Mitanni 166
Mithras 113
Moorish universities 133
Moses 36-7, 41, 44, 109, 128
Moshili 167
Mt. Horeb 114
Mt. Sinai 49
Mt. St. Helens 54, 60
Mt. Tambora 55
Muhammad 108, 128-30,
multi-generational groups 18
mummification 25
Mursili I 164
Muslim 129
Napoleon 7
natural dehydration 22
Nebuchadnezzar II 114
Nefertari 26, 76
Nefertiti 65, 73, 77, 83, 92, 95
Nez Perce 46
Nicene Creed 126
Nile River 12, 15, 21
Noah 108
Nubia 47, 76
Odin 183
Old Hebrew 27
Old Kingdom 34
Old Testament 39, 41-2, 68, 92, 110, 117, 130
orographical map 4
Osiris 35, 75, 156

Osman, Ahmen 71
pantheon of gods 22
paradise 23-5
Patriarchs 127
Paul (Saul) 117, 148
penicillin 21
Pepi II 43
petroglyphs 11
Phoenican language 30, 33
pillar of salt 29
Ponce de Leon 189
Pope Gregory IX 118
Potiphar 63
power of healing 123
predators 20
priesthood 24
Promised Land 28, 46
Ptah 12
Pyramid of Giza 23
Queen Kiya 82, 86, 95
Queen Mutnedjmet 100
Queen Tiye 71-3, 79, 95
Ramesses I 100
Ramesses II 25, 40, 43, 168
Red /Reed Sea 43, 48, 62, 93
resurrection 121
River Styx 147
Roman Emperor Crassus 116?
Roman Empire 117, 122, 132
Rome 116, 125
Sakir-Har 40
Samaritans 115
sanitation 18
Santorini 53-4, 70, 109
Saqqara 18-9
Sarah 28, 107, 129
scribes 11
Semenkhkare 73, 82, 97
Semitic culture 27

Semitic Hyksos 53
Seth 38, 155
Seti I 25
seven fat cows 64
Sheba 112
Shem 108
shepherd king 40
Shi'a 129, 131
Shuppiluluma 83, 166
Shuster, Joe 5
sickle swords 28
Siegel, Jerry 5
slaves 44, 46, 116
smoking pillar 49
Sodom and Gomorrah 28
Spartacus 165-6
Stone Age 16-7
subsistence-level diet 20
subterranean world 23
Sumerian gods 6
Sumerians 171-3
Sunni 129
superheroes 8-9, 18, 109, 224
superhumans 6, 46, 126
Superman 5-6
super-powers 44
superstitions 14
super-villains 8
supreme sacrifices 13
survival skills 13
Syrian Christians 121
Talmud 117-18
Tell el-Amarna 78
Ten Commandments 49
terracotta figurines 18
the American Way 5
the Kaaba 131
Thebes 36, 38
theocracy 36

Thera 54, 59-60, 79, 109, 111
Thor 183
Thutmose IV 71, 79
Thutmose V 72
Tigris, Euphrates Rivers 15, 76
tomb robbers 23-4
Torah 117, 149
transgression against the gods 24
Tutankhamun 43, 72, 81-3, 89, 95-8
universal god 106, 112, 116
Ur 27
Valhalla 150
Valley of the Kings 24
van Leeuwenhoek, Antony 20
Varus, Roman General 122
Vikings 184
Vonnegut, Kurt 134
walking sticks 84
Wylie Coyote 6
Yahweh 107, 115
Zarathustra 112, 150
zero-tech world 8
Zeus 174, 177
ziggurat 27
zygote 126

Hubble Earth View

Courtesy of Hubblesite. org
Space Telescope Science Institute

Superheroes

Giant-Size X-Men #1 from cover of Marvel Comics and published in 1975
©2010 by Marvel Characters, Inc. Used by permission